The Everything Book

The Everything Book

A Treasury of Things for Children to Make and Do

The Everything Book

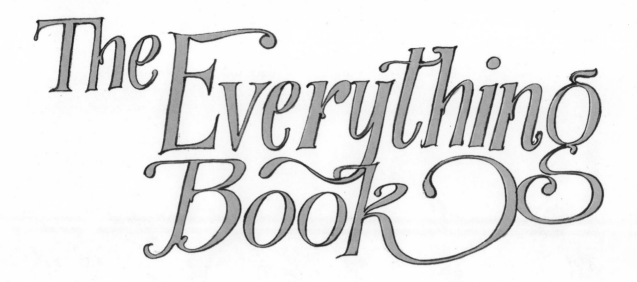

A Treasury of Things for Children to Make and Do

by Eleanor Graham Vance

illustrated by Trina S. Hyman

gb GOLDEN PRESS · NEW YORK
Western Publishing Company, Inc.
Racine, Wisconsin

Dedicated to
everyone who likes children

Grateful acknowledgment is made to Modern Maturity *and to* NRTA
Journal, *in both of which some of the material in this book has previously appeared.*

Contents

PART II

Things to Do

FOREWORD

THE EVERYTHING BOOK will never be finished. It is my hope that each reader will keep on adding to it, making his own special collection of activities that the young and old of his acquaintance can enjoy together.

The book in your hands gives you a sample of things which I have found children enjoy. Anyone who can read can use the book; but I have addressed it to adults rather than to children, because the very young need help not only in carrying out directions but also in assembling materials and cleaning up.

Nearly all materials called for are already available in most households. Finger paint, paste, and all sorts of individual card games can be bought in stores, but children become more resourceful and creative if they learn to "make do" with things around the house. Just as it is more satisfying to know how to use a hammer yourself than to have to pay someone else to use the hammer for you, so it is good for youngsters to be stimulated to create their own fun out of whatever is at hand.

While there are many specific instructions here, I hope you will take off on your own. If you know a better way, do your own thing. If you have your own favorite songs, add them to the ones here. If something I have written reminds you of something you have made or of a game you played, share it with today's children. *The Everything Book* can't really contain "everything," but I hope it will remind you of songs, rhymes, riddles, games, recipes—all kinds of activities you may have forgotten—and give you an alternative to saying, "Go and watch TV."

It is impossible to name all the people who have had a part in this book. Nearly everyone I ever knew has helped in some way. My thanks go back to the only grandmother I ever knew, and to my father and mother, who gave me my love of words. My husband helped with many projects, and put up with me during the long writing hours. Two specialists in early childhood education, Anita LaSueur Vance and Mary Hughes Eder, gave me many valuable suggestions. My daughter, Eleanor Raders, and my daughter-in-law, Beverly Vance, provided me not only with ideas but also with my laboratory: my grandchildren, Lynn, Laura, Jerry, Stephanie, and Mike Raders, and Jay and Katy Vance. To all of these, to many patient librarians, and to my other clever and helpful friends named and unnamed, I say Thank You.

E. G. V.
Edinburg, Texas

9/16/73

Things to Make

Things to Use

For an adult, "things to use" ordinarily serve a practical purpose. For children, some of the very best things to use are things to play with. A newspaper (already "used" as far as the readers in the family are concerned) can be recycled into many interesting things.

NEWSPAPER MAGIC

Paper dolls It is doubtful whether any bought paper dolls give children as much pleasure as the kind they can make for themselves.

Tear a strip about six inches wide from the edge of a double sheet of newspaper. Fold it from end to end, in half, then in fourths, then in eighths, then in sixteenths. (This makes eight dolls. If a child is doing the cutting or

tearing, it's easier to start with four dolls instead of eight.)

Draw on the fold a pattern similar to the picture of half a doll below. Cut or tear on the lines. When you get used to doing this, you won't need to draw a pattern. Finished dolls can remain hand in hand to dance Ring-around-a-Rosy, or they may be torn apart.

At home, the newspaper may serve only as practice to get a good pattern, since children may prefer to go on to better paper for the dolls they want to keep. But away from home, or at any time when plain paper isn't readily available, a newspaper doll can be interesting — especially if there is a pencil or crayon handy to indicate hair and features, collars and belts, buttons and pockets.

At the age of five, Katy loved to cut out the models from pattern booklets her Grandma gave her. She named the "dollies" and put them through endless dramas.

"Stuffed" paper dolls Stuffed paper dolls can be made by cutting out four, six, or eight of the folded dolls on plain white paper, and then cutting them apart to make backs and fronts for two, three, or four dolls.

Draw and color faces and fronts on half of the dolls, backs on the other half. Place a back down, with the colored side facing downward. Put paste or glue on the side that is turned up. Place a thin layer of cotton wadding on that, more glue, and then the front of the doll. Be sure the face is turned up.

Press the back and front together carefully around the edges so the stuffing doesn't show. Then wipe off excess glue.

These dolls will dangle nicely from a thread and can be used to decorate a Christmas tree. Several of them can be combined to make an attractive mobile.

More permanent stuffed dolls can be made of felt.

Clothes for paper dolls (plain or stuffed) Lay the doll on another paper, and draw around the dress or trousers part of the doll. Add shoulder tabs, or, better still, make dresses double by drawing on a paper folded at the top. Be sure to leave front and back connected at the shoulders (to hold the dress on). This kind of pattern is good for clothes made from scraps of cloth.

Remember that children like paper dolls at more than one age. The little ones enjoy making (or even watching them made). At a later stage, they like to design elaborate wardrobes, create backgrounds, and even make up plays for them.

Paper hats Understanding written directions is harder than following what a person does. So try to *show* rather than tell a child how to make these next things.

Hats

1. Take a whole double sheet of newspaper.

2. Fold it in half.

3. Make folds where dotted lines are.

4. Fold point A in to center, and point B in to center.

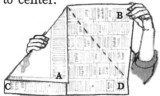

5. Fold edge of CD back up as far as it will go. Turn the edge up on the other side, too.

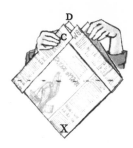

6. Pick up by points C and D; open and bring them together and flatten to a square.

7. Fold the two open points (C and D) back (one on each side) to X. This makes a hat a child can wear. (It makes a larger hat at Step 5, but the hat doesn't hold together as well at that stage.)

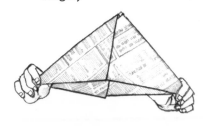

Paper boats Go through the seven steps above, and then repeat 6 and 7. The little hat will have a front part, a back part, and a middle part. Pull the two middle parts gently, grasping one end with the left hand and one with the right. It makes a boat.

A tree that grows Mary Mahan showed us how to do this at the Frick Summer Conference for Teachers at Wilson College.

1. Take a double sheet of newspaper and tear it in half across the middle.

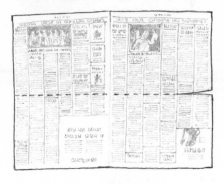

2. Roll one half up into a tube. When you get about 5 inches from the end, add the other half-sheet and roll it into the same tube.

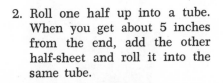

3. Flatten the tube. Tear or cut down from the top about 4 inches. Make four cuts or tears.

4. Then hold the "trunk" of the tree in the left hand, and reach right hand into center "leaves" and coax them gently upward so that the tree "grows." You can also make the tree smaller by coaxing the leaves back down.

Note: You can make this tree with only *one* half of a double sheet — only it won't grow quite so high. Also you can make one that grows still more by rolling in *another* sheet if you can manage to cut or tear through the additional thicknesses to make the leaves. In fact, you can add indefinitely, as long as you can cut through the additions.

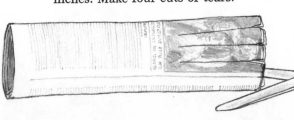

PAPIER MACHÉ

When I showed my outline for this book to one of my friends, she wanted me to leave out papier maché. "It's so messy!" she protested.

Well, I don't mind the mess. I reminded her that cookbook authors don't expect *every* reader to use *every* recipe, but they like to provide for many tastes.

So here — for those who want to try — are two ways to make papier maché. Incidentally, I don't think it's any messier than painting, or some kinds of cooking, or lots of other activities.

For modeling (like clay) Take about 40 sheets of newspaper. (Any quantity can be used, but this is a good amount for a first batch.) Tear or cut them in strips about an inch wide, and then tear up the strips into pieces about an inch square. A pail is a good container to soak them in, and you can tear them right into the pail. Cover the paper with water and let it stand overnight — or for a couple of days.

(If you plan to surprise the children, do the above ahead of time.)

Pour off and squeeze out the extra water. Add about five tablespoons of paste. (The amount is approximate.) Mix the paste into the paper, and knead until the mixture feels like soft clay.

Now it is ready for the children, and can be used in the same ways as clay, to model puppet heads, small animals, fruits, vegetables, dishes — anything they want to do with it. When the papier maché sculpture dries, it can be painted.

For wrapping on a form (I like this kind better) This requires less preparation. Cut or tear the newspaper strips a little narrower. I find about ½- to ¾-inch strips easier to handle.

Put diluted paste (about the consistency of heavy cream) in a flat dish or saucer. Holding a strip of paper by the ends, pull it through the paste until it is pasty all over. Then use it to wrap whatever form you are using. First be sure to grease the form with vegetable shortening or vaseline.

A bowl is a good thing to start with. You can use the inside or the outside for the form. Put the first layer of strips on in one direction, the next layer at right angles to the first, and so on. Use enough layers to make the covering about ¼ inch thick. Set the covered (or lined) form aside to dry. When it is almost dry, carefully lift the covering (or lining) from the bowl, and let it finish drying. Now it can be painted and decorated.

Christmas tree ornaments can be made by wrapping strips around a small orange or a ball. Let the papier maché get partly dry. Then cut with a single-edged razor blade or a sharp paring knife around the middle, lift off, and put the hollow ball back together with a few fresh strips of pasty paper. Paint or spray with glitter.

All kinds of interesting animals can be made by creating forms out of rolled newspaper and wrapping them with the pasty strips, after they have been tied or wired together. We made a pretty good hippopotamus out of a cocoa box turned on its side. Make holes in the side and put small rolls of newspaper in for legs. Use a ball of wadded newspaper for the head (pushed into the open top of the box). Hold everything together with strips of pasty paper.

Homemade Paste A jar of paste is likely to be found in any household, but if you find yourself fresh out of paste, try this recipe:

In a small bowl mix until smooth
   ½ cup flour
   ¼ cup cold water
Over this mixture, pour
   1 cup boiling water

Stir until it takes on a transparent look. Strain it if necessary, and thin it with cold water until it is of the desired consistency.

Of course, you can double or triple the above recipe to make larger amounts, but this is plenty for most activities, and it is better to make a new supply than to keep it too long.

PAPER BAG MAGIC

Let children think of all the things they can do with paper bags. A large one can make a costume for a small child. Masks, puppet heads, etc., can be made from smaller bags.

Masks and puppets Choose a bag that fits the child's head loosely. Put it on over his head, and feel gently with your fingers to see where his eyes, nose, and mouth come on the bag. Mark places with felt marker or crayon. Remove the bag and let the child make bold features with crayons or markers or paints. Cut out eyes so he can see, and cut out mouth so he can stick out his tongue. Let him color the mask as psychedelically as he likes.

VARIATIONS: 1. Stuff smaller bags with crumpled newspaper (after marking features and cutting out eyes and mouth). Cover with papier maché strips. (See page 17.) Leave eye and mouth holes uncovered, or cut them out before strips harden. When dry, paint the face and remove stuffing.

2. Stuff smaller bags with crumpled newspaper. Draw tops together to make a neck, and tie with string. Paint faces. Add hair, etc. These can serve as heads of characters in a puppet play. A piece of cloth is gathered around the "neck" to serve as a dress and to cover the puppeteer's hand.

Costumes Cut a hole in the bottom of a large paper bag, and cut it all the way down one side. (The child must be small, the bag large.) Fit it to the child, make armholes, and then take it off; let him color it and decorate it with buttons, pockets, etc.

Paper tails Audregene Nicely says, "All kids ought to know how to make these. They make tails, arms, legs, etc."

I think these used to be called "cat stairs." They can be made with any kind of paper, but a good source is a large paper bag. Cut down the seam side of the bag, and cut the bottom off the bag. This makes a large rectangle of strong paper. Use it to cut long strips, about an inch wide.

1. Lay the strips on a flat surface, and paste the end of one to the end of the other, at right angles. (Paste is unnecessary, but it holds the two strips in position to get started.)

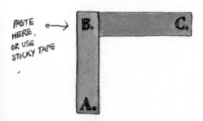

PASTE HERE, OR USE STICKY TAPE

2. Fold strip AB down over strip BC.

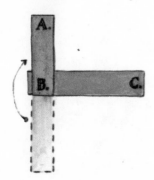

3. Then fold BC back over BA.

Continue folding one and then the other strip over, always keeping the corner square. Once you get started, you don't need the flat surface, but can hold the strips in your hands and continue at a great rate until you come to the end of your strips. If the tail isn't as long as you would like, simply increase to length by adding on strips of the same width.

The above direction, advising the use of one-inch strips, is only for learning. Once you know how, you can make strips any width you like. Some people like to paste the last flap down so the tail won't come apart.

See how many ways you can use these tails.

19

ALUMINUM FOIL

If you use aluminum foil, the tails described on page 19 make good icicles or twinklers for a Christmas tree.

Two 18-inch strips make a twinkler about six inches long.

Foil needs no paste to hold it together, but it's a good idea for an adult (or an older child) to provide the long narrow strips (about ¾ of an inch wide, folded lengthwise to one-half their width). Folding makes them stronger and easier to handle, and also makes the strips shiny on both sides.

With a needle, put a thread through the top to hang the twinkler.

Foil masks Use heavy-duty foil; or if you have none, double a piece of regular foil large enough to cover the child's face. Let him help you smooth and fit the foil closely over his eyes, nose, and mouth to make a perfect mask. Don't flatten the nose, but pinch the foil gently to follow the shape of the child's nose. (It doesn't shut off breathing, because it doesn't cling, and you can lift the foil off every few seconds and put it back in place until you and the child are satisfied.) Remove foil carefully (to keep its shape) and place the mask over a wad of crumpled newspaper while you cover it with papier maché (page 16). This time, tear ½-inch newspaper strips into small pieces, dip them in thin paste, and gently cover the mask with four or five layers of the pasty bits. (You have to be gentle to keep the mask in shape.)

After it is dry, let the child paint it and see how much he can make the life mask look like him.

What else can you make with foil?

PAPER PLATE PUPPETS

Cut across one paper plate, removing the lower third or one-half. Glue or staple this to a whole paper plate (the two plates facing, not nested). The cut-away part makes a pocket for a child's hand. Make a face on the whole plate, and you have a character for a homemade drama.

Impromptu puppet shows can be based on Mother Goose rhymes or nursery tales or comic strip characters.

HANDKERCHIEF MAGIC

Babies in a hammock
1. Fold handkerchief into a triangle.

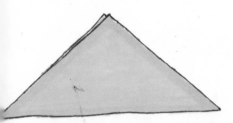

2. Roll right lower corner to middle.

3. Do the same with left lower corner.

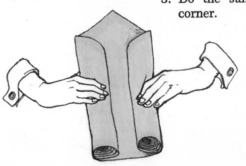

4. Separate top points gently, and bring lower one *under*, to opposite side so that the two small rolls (the babies) appear on the left side and can be swung back and forth.

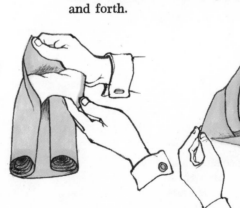

Many a little girl has sat through a dull sermon in church, sustained, strengthened, and *kept quiet* by her knowledge of how to make babies in a hammock out of her mother's handkerchief.

Mr. or Mrs. Hanky Panky

Eleanor Herzog taught me how to make this:

1. Lay handkerchief out flat on a hard surface.

2. Roll each side to the middle.

3. Fold top half over bottom half.

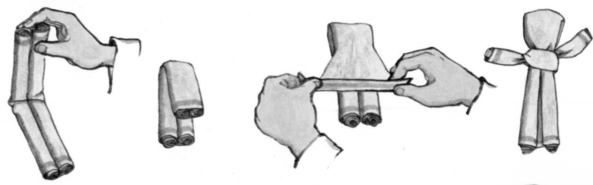

4. Pull top rolls gently to sides and fold back, separating enough to make it possible to tie the ends together around the "doll," to make arms.

> Mr. Hanky Panky makes a nice doll for a little one who is temporarily childless (as for instance, waiting in a doctor's office or riding on a bus).

Mr. Mouse

1. Fold handkerchief into triangle.

2. Turn lower points in, as shown.

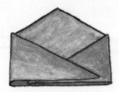

3. Beginning at bottom, fold handkerchief toward top until only a small triangle remains.

4. Lay left hand, palm-side up, on folded handkerchief.

5. Turn top triangle down and hold it between fingers.

6. Turn each end in and hold all together with thumb. Then take right hand and twist handkerchief from back of left-hand fingers to front, always twisting in same direction, and moving left-hand thumb and fingers in order to allow all the back part of the handkerchief to be twisted over the front part.

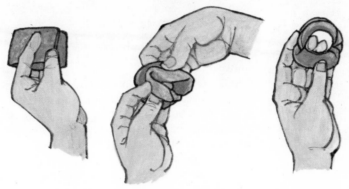

7. Coax out the ends.

8. If one end is longer than the other, choose it for the mouse's head. Take this end, pull it sideways, and twist to tie into ears.

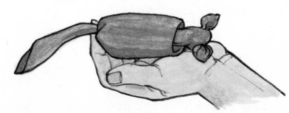

The mouse can jump if you hold your hand cupped and lay the mouse on top with the head lying at base of your thumb, and the tail end of body just where the fingertips of your curled fingers are. Then when the hand is closed convulsively, the mouse will jump. Small children just like to *throw* him.

Al Heymann taught me how to make a mouse more than thirty-five years ago. Since then I may have made 50,-000 mice.

Note: Don't tell children immediately that if you pull the head and tail simultaneously, the mouse turns back into a handkerchief, because then you will have to make mouse after mouse. But if they are learning how to make it themselves, then you can tell them.

DRAWING AND PAINTING

Most mothers don't feel equipped to be art teachers, and there's no reason why they should. The important thing is to supply the children with plenty of materials and let them experiment. They will be more creative if you give them plenty of interest in — and appreciation of — what they are doing, and a minimum of direction about how to do it. When they bring you the finished product, of course you won't ask, "What's that supposed to be?" But perhaps you'll want to say, "Tell me about your picture," or just "How beautiful!"

Arthur Guiterman once told me a story about a little girl who announced to her mother, "I'm drawing a picture of a birdie in a cage." The mother looked at the picture and said, "I see the cage, but where is the bird." "Oh," said the young artist imperturbably as she went on with her work, "the birdie's in the pencil yet."

Nowadays, some of the "experts" tell us we shouldn't ask, "Where is the bird?" But I have always loved that story because it shows how the artist's idea can be so real to him that he feels he's *liberating* something already there.

Naturally, you make some suggestions by the very materials you supply. Make these as varied as you can. Pencils and crayons are found in every home. Add paints if possible. If there is no paint in the house, remember that food coloring makes a good watercolor for painting on paper. Add a very small amount of egg yolk and powdered detergent to food color, and it will stick to shiny surfaces like glass or egg cartons or aluminum foil.

Some suggestions follow for equipment to supply young artists.

For spatter painting: A piece of screen, an old toothbrush, pins, paper, leaves or original cut-outs.

For string pictures: Bowls of any kind of paint and short lengths of string. Dip string in paint. Let it fall on paper. Even the youngest will enjoy this.

For eggshell mosaics: Eggshells, food color, paper, and glue. If you are making any egg dish, it is easy to save the shells. Let the children color them several different shades with food color, and spread them out to dry. When they are dry, they are ready for

making eggshell mosaics. Your artists may want to make a flower or a geometric design before they attempt anything as elaborate as a landscape. It is a good idea to keep the bits of shell in separate piles of different colors — blue here, yellow there. Children often prefer to draw their whole picture with a pencil, and then spread glue and shells over small areas at a time. Keep a damp washcloth handy to wipe glue from fingers.

Susan Zivkovic reminds me that mosaics can also be made with cut or torn bits of colored paper.

FINGER PAINTING

Recipe for homemade finger paint:

Pour bottled liquid starch in small quantities into two or three containers (jar lids or saucers — or small jars if you want to keep the paint for future sessions). Put a few drops of food color into each container while Johnny stirs with his finger and decides when the desired shade is reached. It is a good idea to start with the primary colors, red, blue, and yellow, and then show Johnny (or let him find out for himself) that red and yellow make orange, blue and yellow make green, and red, blue, and yellow make brown.

You can make a big hit if you suggest that you would like to have a "mural" on the refrigerator. Your little artists will be quick to respond. (Mine couldn't believe their ears when I first mentioned it.) Enameled metal tabletops or surfaces covered with laminated plastic like Formica or Micarta are also possibilities for finger painting. If you don't believe that starch tinted with food color wipes right off with a wet rag, try it for yourself on a small spot. The finger paint spreads more easily if the surface is wet.

Visiting children will understand that if they want to *keep* their pictures to take home, they must make them on wet shelf paper. Nevertheless, decorating a refrigerator can be a lot of fun.

"Real" finger painting means covering the wet paper with paint and then using the whole hand to move it around and create swirls or lines or patterns, but I let my little artists use only one finger if they want to.

OTHER HINTS

Coffee grounds or sand mixed with paint will produce different textures. If you can't find a paint brush, try a Q-tip, a feather, or a piece of cotton wound around a toothpick or pencil. Make paint by adding dry color to thin paste.

Remember that grandparents are ardent collectors of young art. Cathy, Suzy, and Tom have a faraway Nana and a faraway Mimi who love to get their pictures in the mail.

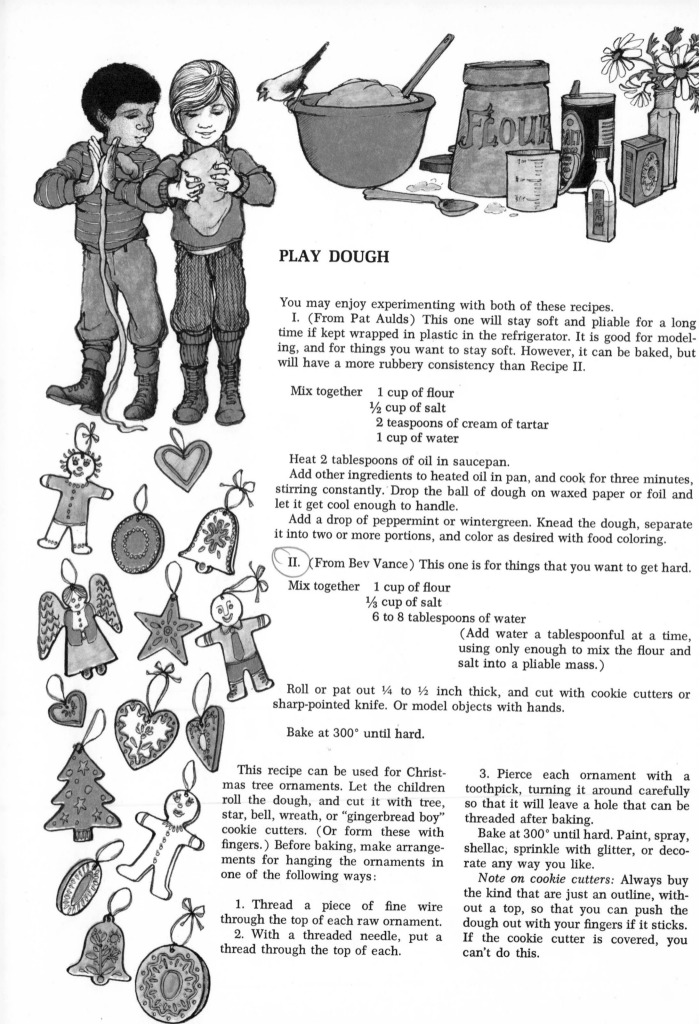

PLAY DOUGH

You may enjoy experimenting with both of these recipes.

I. (From Pat Aulds) This one will stay soft and pliable for a long time if kept wrapped in plastic in the refrigerator. It is good for modeling, and for things you want to stay soft. However, it can be baked, but will have a more rubbery consistency than Recipe II.

Mix together   1 cup of flour
½ cup of salt
2 teaspoons of cream of tartar
1 cup of water

Heat 2 tablespoons of oil in saucepan.

Add other ingredients to heated oil in pan, and cook for three minutes, stirring constantly. Drop the ball of dough on waxed paper or foil and let it get cool enough to handle.

Add a drop of peppermint or wintergreen. Knead the dough, separate it into two or more portions, and color as desired with food coloring.

II. (From Bev Vance) This one is for things that you want to get hard.

Mix together   1 cup of flour
⅓ cup of salt
6 to 8 tablespoons of water

> (Add water a tablespoonful at a time, using only enough to mix the flour and salt into a pliable mass.)

Roll or pat out ¼ to ½ inch thick, and cut with cookie cutters or sharp-pointed knife. Or model objects with hands.

Bake at 300° until hard.

This recipe can be used for Christmas tree ornaments. Let the children roll the dough, and cut it with tree, star, bell, wreath, or "gingerbread boy" cookie cutters. (Or form these with fingers.) Before baking, make arrangements for hanging the ornaments in one of the following ways:

1. Thread a piece of fine wire through the top of each raw ornament.
2. With a threaded needle, put a thread through the top of each.

3. Pierce each ornament with a toothpick, turning it around carefully so that it will leave a hole that can be threaded after baking.

Bake at 300° until hard. Paint, spray, shellac; sprinkle with glitter, or decorate any way you like.

Note on cookie cutters: Always buy the kind that are just an outline, without a top, so that you can push the dough out with your fingers if it sticks. If the cookie cutter is covered, you can't do this.

HAND PRINTS

In its simplest form, a hand print is just a colored outline of a little hand and can be made in a few minutes. Get Johnny to lay his hand flat (with fingers spread wide) on a sheet of paper. Draw around it with a pencil (or help him to do it with his other hand). Then Johnny can make the outline heavier with a dark crayon, and fill in any color he likes. He may want to cut out the hand and mount it on another sheet of paper. He can give this away as a present to Mother or Grandmother, or he can keep it in his room till next year to see how fast his hand grows.

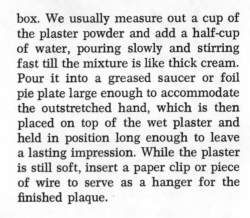

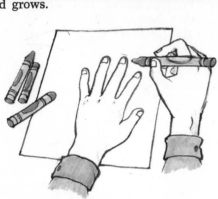

A more ambitious project is to draw the hand print on cloth, and then appliqué it onto a pot holder. (One mother did this as a gift for her child's Sunday school teacher.) Or embroider it in chain or outline stitch on material that can be made into a pot holder, doily, or picture to hang on the wall.

The most exciting hand prints are made of plaster of Paris, which can be bought by the pound in a hardware store. Directions for mixing are on the box. We usually measure out a cup of the plaster powder and add a half-cup of water, pouring slowly and stirring fast till the mixture is like thick cream. Pour it into a greased saucer or foil pie plate large enough to accommodate the outstretched hand, which is then placed on top of the wet plaster and held in position long enough to leave a lasting impression. While the plaster is still soft, insert a paper clip or piece of wire to serve as a hanger for the finished plaque.

Variation: Leaf prints Gather several different kinds of leaves (not too big). Place each leaf (or a group of two or three if there is room) in the bottom of the container, face down. Cottage cheese cartons or greased foil pie pans are good containers. Pour plaster of Paris (mixed as above for hand prints) on top of leaves to a depth of about a quarter-inch. When plaster begins to set, take a sharp paring knife and cut a small slit near the bottom of the container to make possible the insertion of the paper clip hanger into the plaque. When hardening is complete, cut down the side of the container at the place where the hanger is, and peel off the container. Take the leaves off the plaster and paint the impression.

If you want to make leaf and hand prints at the same time, get everything ready before mixing the plaster. Then pour the plaster for the leaf prints first, because the owner of the hand has to stand still until the plaster sets enough to hold the impression.

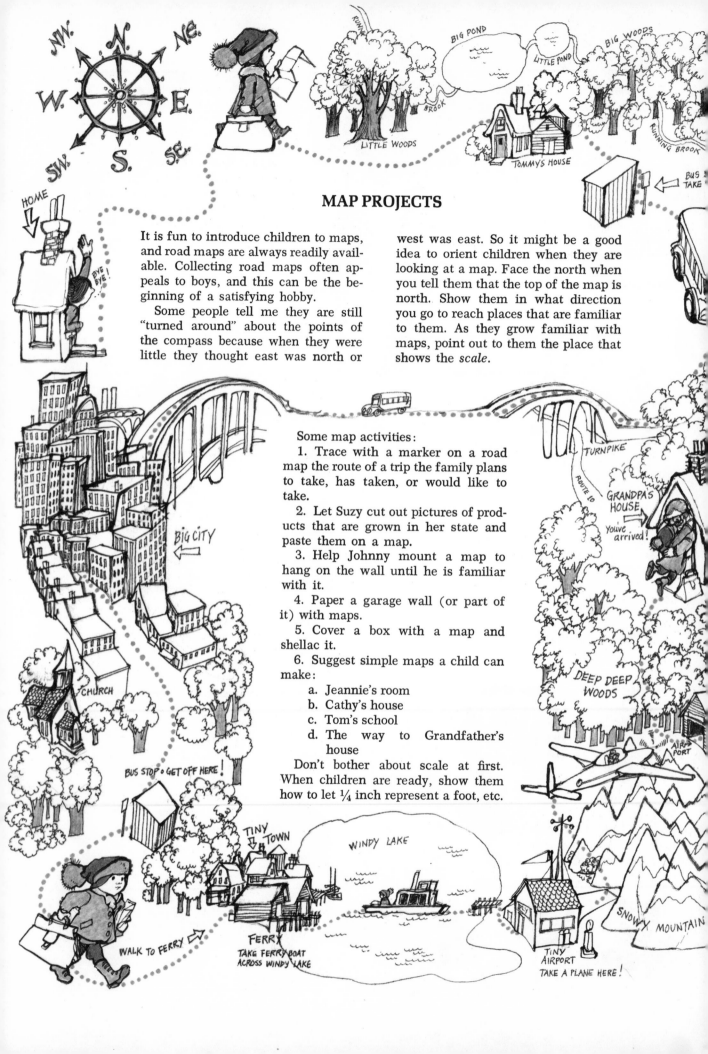

MAP PROJECTS

It is fun to introduce children to maps, and road maps are always readily available. Collecting road maps often appeals to boys, and this can be the beginning of a satisfying hobby.

Some people tell me they are still "turned around" about the points of the compass because when they were little they thought east was north or west was east. So it might be a good idea to orient children when they are looking at a map. Face the north when you tell them that the top of the map is north. Show them in what direction you go to reach places that are familiar to them. As they grow familiar with maps, point out to them the place that shows the *scale*.

Some map activities:

1. Trace with a marker on a road map the route of a trip the family plans to take, has taken, or would like to take.

2. Let Suzy cut out pictures of products that are grown in her state and paste them on a map.

3. Help Johnny mount a map to hang on the wall until he is familiar with it.

4. Paper a garage wall (or part of it) with maps.

5. Cover a box with a map and shellac it.

6. Suggest simple maps a child can make:

   a. Jeannie's room
   b. Cathy's house
   c. Tom's school
   d. The way to Grandfather's house

Don't bother about scale at first. When children are ready, show them how to let ¼ inch represent a foot, etc.

PICTURES FROM BUTTONS, SEEDS, AND SIMILAR MATERIALS

My button box, inherited from Mother and added to (as well as subtracted from) through the years, has provided many hours of enjoyment for several generations of children. Even ordinary buttons from old shirts are useful in pictures or for "building materials" when you are making "streets" on the floor.

Occasionally we use a few buttons, along with seeds from canteloupe and watermelon, bits of ribbon and braid, dried sea oats and grasses, pieces of eggshell, and the like, to make a collage. Let your little artist arrange and rearrange until he finds a composition to his liking, and then he can glue the things in place. He may want to make a realistic picture, or an abstract.

But long before children have reached this stage, they like to use the buttons for *im*permanent pictures — those that are produced simply by arranging the buttons to make a picture or design, and then putting them away until the next time. This can be done on the floor or on a table, but it helps the artist to limit his picture if you give him a sheet of paper or cardboard to work on.

DECORATED EGGS AND EGGSHELLS

Everyone is familiar with dyed hard-boiled eggs for Easter. This is something easy to do, and children enjoy taking part in it. If you want to invest a little extra time, imagination, and patience you can make eggshells into works of art that families will want to keep from year to year.

If you are going to keep them, of course the eggs have to be removed from the shells. With a large needle or a sharp-pointed paring knife, pick a hole in one end of an egg. This hole can be as big as ¼ inch in diameter. In the other end of the egg, simply work the needle in and draw it out. Blow into the tiny hole and let the contents of the egg come out the large one. (If both holes are too tiny, it takes forever to blow out the egg.) Holes can later be covered with a piece of cellophane adhesive tape or with decorative materials.

If you prepare several shells at one time, you can use the contents for scrambled eggs.

Wash the emptied shells carefully and stand them in an egg box to dry. Now they are ready for decoration with faces, flower designs, or whatever you like. With the addition of hats, collars, hair, and such, you can make a variety of characters, comic, romantic, or what-have-you.

To thread them for hanging, use a long needle (longer than the egg), and pass it through the egg — in at the small hole and out at the larger one. A small button sewed onto the end of the thread acts as a knot to hold the thread in place. Or try tying a thread around a half-inch of toothpick, and placing a little glue on the ends of the toothpick. Put the toothpick endwise into the hole in the egg, and when it has disappeared inside, pull back gently on the thread to lodge the toothpick crosswise. Even if the glue shouldn't hold, the toothpick has to stay in place. If the egg has yarn hair or a decoration at the top, the easiest way to hang it is to sew a thread loop to whatever is at the top.

Some people use decorated eggshells for Christmas tree ornaments, painting in bright colors or spraying with glitter to suit the season.

My daughter's family has an Easter Egg Tree every year. They bring in a branch of a tree from the yard and deck it with their creations. As the children grow older, they make new ones to add to their collection.

My sister-in-law, Lillian, creates something like a tiny diorama inside an eggshell. She cuts a hole in the side of the shell (sometimes lengthwise, sometimes crosswise) and pours a little melted wax in the bottom to hold the scene in place. Then working with tweezers, she arranges tiny figures, houses, flowers, and scenery cut from greeting cards. Sometimes an infinitesimal bird is suspended from the top by an almost invisible thread so that he actually seems to be flying. The eggs are mounted on plastic curtain rings. All of this requires too much concentration and coordination for a child, but one who is growing up might enjoy an art in which he can create a tiny world inside a shell.

STILTS (out of two 46-ounce cans)

Punch a hole on each side of two 46-ounce juice cans as close to one end of the can as possible. Put strong twine or rope through the holes, leaving enough to tie around a child's feet.

If you use paint cans that have handles, you can simply tie a string to the handle. The trick, of course, is for the child to pull on the string and lift his foot at the same time.

These make good beginner's stilts, since they don't raise your hero too high off the ground, but you had better lay down ground rules that they are for outdoors only, since the cans may be hard on floors or carpets.

LITTLE BOOKS

A small child likes a little book made just for him. Fold a sheet of paper in half, crosswise, and cut. Lay one half on top of the other and fold again, making a little 8-page book. (If he wants more pages, you can add them.) A few stitches (or a staple or two) on the fold will hold the book together.

Let the young author dictate a story to go in the book. Leave room for him to illustrate it with his own drawings or with pictures cut from magazines. Or let him make the pictures first, and then think up a story to go with them. (Don't be surprised if there is not much connection between story and pictures in the beginning.)

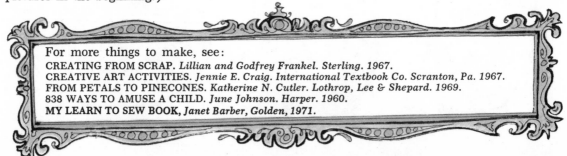

For more things to make, see:
CREATING FROM SCRAP. *Lillian and Godfrey Frankel. Sterling. 1967.*
CREATIVE ART ACTIVITIES. *Jennie E. Craig. International Textbook Co. Scranton, Pa. 1967.*
FROM PETALS TO PINECONES. *Katherine N. Cutler. Lothrop, Lee & Shepard. 1969.*
838 WAYS TO AMUSE A CHILD. *June Johnson. Harper. 1960.*
MY LEARN TO SEW BOOK, *Janet Barber, Golden, 1971.*

Things to Give

Not what we give but what we share,
For the gift without the giver is bare.
James Russell Lowell

Several of the things we have already talked about making (for instance, hand prints, leaf prints, and ornaments made of play dough and papier maché) are good presents for children to give for Christmas or birthdays. Other suggestions are given below.

PLASTIC PILL BOTTLES

Because of its strength and light weight a plastic pill bottle makes an ideal foundation for a little doll — especially one for a collection or for exhibition purposes. Small heads can be bought at a novelty store, but it's more fun to make your own (in the manner given on this page for Mrs. Clean).

Supply scraps of cloth (felt, nylon net — as much variety as possible), and let children devise costumes for an angel, a dancer, an old-fashioned girl, children of other lands, etc.

Pill bottles come in many sizes. Can you think of other things to make with them?

KITCHEN DOLL

A plastic bottle full of dishwashing detergent can be "dressed" in a couple of new dishrags to make a useful kitchen doll for Auntie or Grandma. Wrinkle newspaper into a ball to make a head. Practice two or three times to get the right size. Or use a Styrofoam ball instead (but I prefer the newspaper method, because paper is always at hand). Tie a square of soft cloth (an old hankie or a piece of sheet) around the paper, and then tie this securely around the stopper of the bottle. Make eyes, nose, and mouth with a brush dipped in food coloring, with paint, or with markers. If the head wobbles, the shawl will help to hold it in place. Use one dishrag as a head shawl, tying it around the neck with string; the other as a skirt. If you have time, you can gather the skirt loosely. If not, just wrap and tie with string or yarn. A pastry brush can be tied on at the waist to serve as a broom for "Mrs. Clean."

DISH (OR BATHTUB) CLEANER

Like some women, nylon net is delicate in appearance, yet tough and durable. Choose pastel shades to go with kitchen or bathroom colors. Cut five or six strips five inches wide and 18 inches long. (Four is enough if your net is in short supply, but more layers make for greater durability in the finished product.)

Lay the strips one on top of the other and pin them in place. With strong durable thread, gather the strips down the middle (lengthwise), pull the gathers as tight as possible, and sew firmly. Fluff out the net layers to make a ball.

Cut and pin the strips for children, but let them do the gathering themselves if they are able. If you have to do it yourself, even a very small child likes to pull the needle through, provided you have the time to be patient.

BATH SALTS

Buy Epsom salts in bulk. Measure out the amount needed to fill whatever bottles you are going to use. (Use plastic pill bottles, small apothecary jars from the Five-and-Ten, baby-food jars, or any clear bottle.) It is a good idea to put the amount of salts for each container in a separate saucer or plate, so that the children can make a variety of tints. Use food color to dye the salts, stirring in a drop at a time until the desired shade is reached. After the salts are returned to the jars, put a drop or two of good perfume or cologne into each container.

The containers can be painted with flowers, decorated with ribbon or felt scraps, or ornamented in any way you like. The small bottles furnish just enough for one bath, and the larger ones are pretty enough to remain in the bathroom until they are used up.

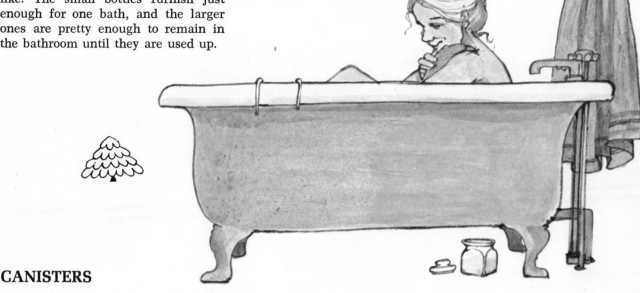

CANISTERS

A one-pound coffee can, a two-pound coffee can, and a three-pound shortening can will make a good set of canisters. One child can make all three, or three children can work on them at once.

Provide materials and offer suggestions, but let the children work out their own creations. One way is to cover a coffee can with aluminum foil, and unroll the right type of plastic dish cleaner over it. Decorated plastic with adhesive backing makes a good covering material. So does felt, but it must be glued on. Boys often prefer to paint the cans rather than cover them.

(Another project can be making cookies to put in the canisters.)

Small cans (the ones that originally held frozen fruit juices or tomato paste or tomato sauce) can be made into pencil holders for a desk.

VARIATION: Children can make faces on the cans, adding yarn hair, paper hats (that are removable), arms, and legs. These make amusing decorations to put on a shelf in Brother's or Sister's room, where they also serve as caddies for small treasures.

PUZZLES

Let children search through old magazines for a bright, colorful picture to
paste on cardboard and cut into pieces
to make a puzzle. Supervise both the
pasting and the cutting, as the puzzle
will not be any fun if it is not well
made. The paste or glue must be
spread over the entire surface, and
the cutting must be careful so that the
pieces will fit back together perfectly.
There is a knack to cutting for a puzzle.
Practice on a plain piece of cardboard.
A whole puzzle of square pieces would-
n't be any fun at all, and too *many*
small pieces of cardboard would make
the assembling tedious.

A plain six-inch square of cardboard,
colored with paint or crayon, can be
speedily made into a good quick puzzle.
(A different color on each side makes
the puzzle easier to put back together.)
With a ruler, draw two intersecting
lines, as shown at the right.

Cut the cardboard apart on the lines
shown in the sketch, making four
pieces. The point is to put them back
into a perfect square.

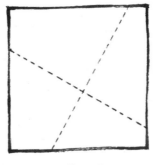

Or draw a T on a cardboard square
and mark it for cutting into four pieces
as shown. Provide a separate envelope
in which to store each puzzle. (The
shaded portions are not part of the
puzzle and are discarded.)

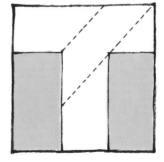

BOOKMARKS

These can be made out of many materials. Provide scraps of felt, oil cloth,
plastic, leather, burlap strips, wall paper, old greeting cards, yarn, paste,
glue, pencils, crayons, and paints.
Make suggestions if children need
them, but remember that no one is
overcritical of a gift made with love.
However, you don't do a child a favor
by praising sloppy work, and most children like to be helped to do their best.

PICTURES ON WOOD

These are made from scrap wood. (Sometimes you can get scrap where a house is being built.) A picture is painted or crayoned on the surface. Many small artists feel that wood gives their creations more permanence — and it really does.

BRICK GARDEN

Place some pieces of brick — or charcoal briquets, or coal — in a shallow bowl or foil pie plate. If you want to enhance the garden effect, glue some small twigs in among the brick pieces. While the glue is hardening, mix together in a separate bowl:

6 tablespoon salt
6 tablespoon bluing
6 tablespoon water
1 tablespoon household ammonia

Pour this mixture over the brick pieces. Each day add a teaspoon of ammonia. As flowerets appear, let children tint them with food coloring. (Put the food coloring in the ammonia if you don't want it too bright.) It's fun to watch the changes from day to day.

COME BACK

A good present to make for a little brother or sister is a comeback.

Take a one-pound coffee can and punch a hole in the center of the bottom and in the center of the top. Stretch a strong rubber band through from bottom to top, fastening it with a piece of toothpick at each end. In the middle of the rubber band, tie a weight (a small rock or a piece of metal). Paint or decorate the can as you like.

When the can is rolled away from you, it will come back.

ROCK ANIMALS AND PEOPLE
(to serve as paperweights,
ornaments, or toys)

Take children for a walk, each one carrying his own paper bag. Let them gather small rocks with interesting shapes. Tell them you are going to use them to make animals and people, so they can be thinking of this when they gather the rocks. Provide glue and paint and yarn and scraps of felt or cloth. Encourage the children to try various combinations to be sure they have constructed the creature they want before they glue it.

If the creature is to be used on a desk, glue felt on the bottom so that the rock won't scratch.

Some parts of the country have more rock than others. Look for them when you travel.

When I was a little girl, we liked to find a "lucky stone" — a small smooth stone that is comfortable to carry in the hand or in the pocket.

DECORATED NOTE PAPER

Buy a box of plain note paper at the
Five-and-Ten, or make your own out
of typewriting paper that has been
cut and folded to fit extra envelopes
you may have from an old box of
stationery.

Get the children to collect tiny fresh
flowers, or use pressed ones. The tip of
a fern, some tiny leaves, or grasses will
do. Place a spray in the upper lefthand
corner of the stationery, and cut a
piece of clear adhesive-backed plastic
that will completely cover the little
arrangement and hold it in place.

CUSTOM-MADE
CARDS AND GIFTS

Homemade cards for birthday, Christmas, or any holiday can be fashioned
in a short time and are as much ap-
preciated as any gift — especially by
parents, grandparents, and other close
relatives.

When Laura was six she drew a
picture of Abraham Lincoln for Grandfather's February birthday. It became
one of Grandfather's prized posses-
sions, but Laura grew increasingly
critical of her gift, and so at 11 she
painted another Lincoln portrait. Perhaps at 16 she will do another.

It often takes just a word from an
adult to make a child realize that by
sharing a talent or hobby, he can
create a gift that no one else can give.
No matter what it is, it is a gift of time
and love.

39

Things to Eat

Speaking of children, Mother used to say, "When you don't know what else to do with them, feed them. That is the first rule of child psychology."

And now nutritionists tell us that when our blood sugar gets low, we become irritable. So a timely snack is a good idea for everybody. Here are a few "kid foods" that are quick and easy to prepare, and simple enough for children to help with.

Let's begin with the staff of life. Most people buy their bread at the store nowadays, but the aroma of baking bread is something to remember for a lifetime, so I hope you will try homemade bread once in a while. Of course, you will have to stay at home for four or five hours (that makes it a good thing to do on a rainy day). But the process is not actually very time-consuming. Most of the time you can be busy with other things, just waiting for the rising, with a timer set to remind you of the bread.

Youngsters love to get their hands into the dough and make their own little loaves. With freshly scrubbed hands, they can do as well as you, if you show them something about kneading.

Use your favorite bread recipe, or look in any cookbook. Don't let a lack of bread pans deter you. One-pound coffee cans are an excellent substitute. Grease them with a solid vegetable shortening, and fill them a little less than half-full with a ball of dough.

Kneading is the real fun, for yeast is *alive*, and handling the dough is handling a living thing. I hope there will always be people who want to introduce John and Mary to the mysteries of bread-making, for it seems to me that handling the living, growing, yeasty creation teaches something about life. The semantics of making bread is revealing: Too much heat too soon can *kill* the yeast. The yeast *feeds* on sugar and *grows* (rises), taking the bread with it. And anyone who has kneaded dough knows he has been in intimate touch with life.

CAKE AND COOKIES

Here's a recipe you may not find in your cookbooks:

Crazy cake (from Lela Priestley)
Directly into an 8-inch square cake pan
    Sift 1½ cups flour
           1 cup sugar
           3 tablespoons cocoa
           1½ teaspoons baking soda
           ½ teaspoon salt
Make three holes in these dry ingredients.
Into one pour 1 teaspoon vanilla.
Into another pour 6 tablespoons cooking oil.
Into the third pour 1 tablespoon vinegar.
Pour 1 cup cold water over all, and beat with a fork until smooth.
Bake at 350° for 25 to 30 minutes.
    Children like this because it is quick and easy and good, and there is nothing to wash but the pan and the measuring things. They also think the name is appropriate because it seems "crazy" to put oil and vinegar in a cake.

Unbaked chocolate oatmeal cookies (from Hazel LaFever)
    2 cups sugar
    6 tablespoons cocoa
    1 stick margarine (¼ lb. or ½ cup)
    ½ cup milk
    pinch of salt
    vanilla if desired
    3 cups raw rolled oats (quick-cooking kind)
    Mix first five ingredients and heat, stirring constantly. Let mixture boil three minutes. (Show children time on a clock, or let them set a timer.) Remove from heat, add vanilla, and stir in rolled oats. Drop by spoonfuls onto waxed paper.
    These are popular — one reason being that it takes no more than thirty minutes from idea to four dozen cookies.

Quick butter cookies (from Joyce Andrews)
   1 stick margarine at room temperature
   1 cup flour
   4 tablespoons sugar
   ¼ teaspoon salt
   1 teaspoon vanilla

Mix softened margarine and other ingredients with a fork or with fingers. Roll into balls about one inch in diameter. Place on cookie sheet and press down with fork, making crisscross pattern. Bake at 350° for ten minutes. Makes about 24.

Since this is a small recipe, it can be put together quickly. However, it can be doubled if necessary.

Oatmeal refrigerator cookies
   In a large bowl, cream 1 cup shortening
                          1 cup white sugar
                   Add   1 cup brown sugar
                          2 eggs
                          1 teaspoon vanilla or almond extract (or ½
                             teaspoon of each)
On a large sheet of waxed paper,
   sift together 2 cups flour
                  ½ teaspoon salt
                  1 teaspoon baking soda
          Add   3 cups quick-cooking rolled oats
                  ½ cup chopped nuts (optional)

Add dry ingredients to creamed mixture and mix well. Shape into rolls about 6 inches long. (Short rolls help to insure against warming up during slicing.) Wrap in waxed paper or foil. Store in refrigerator to use as needed. Take out a roll at a time, slice as thin as possible, and bake about 12 minutes at 375°.

Remember that rolls of refrigerator-cookie dough can also be bought at the supermarket. (These are longer, so slice half a roll at a time.) Children can still have the fun of seeing them bake, and it's a quick way to get that fresh homemade taste without starting from scratch.

Gingerbread boys

In a large bowl, cream together   1 stick margarine (¼ lb. or ½ cup)
                                                  ½ cup white or brown sugar
                            Add   1 egg
                                                  ½ cup molasses

On a large sheet of waxed paper
                           Sift   3½ cups flour
                                                  1 teaspoon soda
                                                  ½ teaspoon salt
                                                  1 teaspoon ginger
                                                  1 teaspoon cinnamon
                                                  ½ teaspoon nutmeg
                                                  ¼ teaspoon cloves
                   Put in a cup   4 tablespoons water

Add about a third of the dry ingredients and half the water to the creamed mixture. Add half the rest of the dry ingredients and the rest of the water, and then the last of the dry ingredients (which you will have to work in with your hands). You may need a little more water to work in all the dry ingredients. Chill the dough.

If the children are very small, everyone scrubs hands, and each one fashions his own little gingerbread boy by rolling a ball for a head, a larger ball for a body, and little rolls for arms and legs, and pressing them together on a greased cookie sheet.

Older children may prefer to make a pattern like the illustration of the paper-doll patterns on page 12, or they may make their own. Cut patterns out of newspaper until you get one you like. Then trace it on cardboard and cut it out.

Roll a portion of chilled dough one-fourth inch thick. Grease the cardboard pattern, lay it on dough, and cut around it with the tip of a paring knife or a pastry wheel. Lift the gingerbread boy by sliding a pancake turner or spatula under it. Children will need help with this. If an arm or a leg breaks off, stick it back on with a little extra dough worked in at the break. Bake on a greased sheet at 350° for 10 to 15 minutes (according to thickness), until firm to the touch. Makes about two dozen 6-inch gingerbread boys.

Raisin eyes can be put in before baking, or children can paint on eyes and other features and decorations afterward. Use the following icing for this:

1 cup confectioners' sugar
1 tablespoon water (more if needed)

Mix this and separate it into several small containers (jar lids, for instance) so that red, blue, and yellow (or any desired color) food coloring can be added. Use a toothpick or a small knife to apply the icing.

MISCELLANEOUS SNACKS

Toasted things If you have an indoor or outdoor fireplace, you are all set up for toasting frankfurters or marshmallows. But a fireplace isn't absolutely necessary. Children can hold a hot dog or marshmallow on a fork over a burner on a kitchen range. Show them that this is also a quick way to loosen the skin of a tomato so that it can be easily peeled. (An adult should be nearby when children work at an open flame.)

A simple meal can be made cooperatively if an adult prepares a canned soup while the children toast hot dogs or make hamburgers. Toasted marshmallows (on crackers or by themselves) serve as dessert. Nutritionists tell us to go easy on hot dogs because of too much fat. (Maybe the meat packers will take the hint and make *lean* frankfurters.)

Help children to improvise homemade and original snacks out of everyday food. For instance, *Toast Fingers* can be made in various ways. Cut slices of bread into strips or "fingers." Mary Jo's mother and dad cut the slices into fourths and called them *Party Squares*.

Brush with melted margarine and grated cheese or coconut or cinnamon and sugar or grated chocolate. Place on cookie sheet and bake at 375° for 10 minutes. Or pop them under the broiler.

Quick homemade pizzas

> 2 lb. ground beef
> 1 teaspoon salt
> 2 8-oz. can refrigerated biscuits (20 biscuits)
> Whatever "fixings" you like or have on hand: Pizza sauce or tomato sauce, grated mozzarella or other cheese, mushrooms, tomato slices, anchovies, etc.

Sprinkle half of salt in skillet. Brown meat and add remaining salt. If there is fat in the pan, pour it off. Roll biscuits to circles of 4 or 5 inches. Place on cookie sheet. Top each biscuit with pizza sauce, beef, and whatever else you like. Children can make their own individual combinations. Bake at 400° for 10 to 12 minutes. Makes 20 small pizzas.

Popcorn From Halloween until Easter, popcorn making and eating are popular occupations. There is no reason popcorn can't be made all year round, but it seems to taste better in cool weather. You will need:

> ⅓ cup raw popcorn
> 3 tablespoons vegetable oil
> Salt to taste

Popcorn may be made in an old-fashioned wire popper over an open fire, in a modern electric popper, or in a heavy iron skillet. In any case, don't try to make too much at once. Electric poppers give their own instructions, but if you are using a skillet or a wire popper, cover the bottom with only a thin layer of corn for each popping. Keep shaking so that the bottom layer

44

Since cooking involves many potential dangers, most parents like to make strict "house rules" that youngsters embark on culinary adventures *only when an adult is available* in case of an emergency.

GELATIN

Gelatin salads and desserts are popular with children, and quick and easy to make. With or without added fruit, cottage cheese, cream cheese, etc., they are good energy foods. There are many recipes on the packages sold at supermarkets.

SPECIAL FRUIT SALAD KIDS CAN MAKE

Use half a peach or a pear (canned or fresh) for a face.

Make eyes, nose, and mouth with cloves, raisins, small cheese cutouts, or pieces of olive or pimiento.

A lettuce leaf can be a skirt; and celery or carrot strips make arms and legs.

Let each child make his own —and eat it.

doesn't burn. Just as it comes from the popper, with nothing added, it makes a good low-fat food. If you make it in a wire popper, you may want to add a little melted margarine or vegetable oil and sprinkle lightly with salt.

Drinks Since soft drinks (because of sugar, which is bad for teeth) and whole milk (because of fat) are frowned upon, teach children to make milkshakes with powdered or skim milk. Dry milk plus water can be substituted for the whole milk in most recipes. If children are introduced to low-fat milk at an early age, they can develop a taste for it. (I know a doctor who says his grown children have never tasted whole milk or butter, and he thinks this diet habit will give them longer, healthier lives.) If your children don't like low-fat milk, you can try to convert them by showing them how to make milkshakes with dry skim milk and water blended with ice milk and a naturally sweet fruit — like bananas, stewed apricots, or prunes.

Raw vegetables Keep celery and carrots on hand. Cut them into thin slivers to make them easier for small teeth to chew, and as soon as children are able, let them learn how to cut the slivers for themselves. This is a good way to teach how to handle a knife. If your Anne lays the carrot on a cutting board and uses the knife always turned with the sharp side toward the carrot and the board, the only thing left to teach her is how to keep the fingers of her holding hand out of the way of the blade.

For more recipes, see:
BETTY CROCKER'S NEW BOYS AND GIRLS COOK BOOK. *Western. 1965.*
THE A TO Z NO-COOK COOKBOOK. *Western. 1974.*

Games

I have concentrated on indoor games, because it is when indoors that an adult is usually looking for ways to entertain children.

VARIATIONS OF HIDE-AND-SEEK

Hiding an object A small child enjoys hiding a ball, a book, a doll, or a stuffed animal instead of himself, and there are always more places to hide an object than to hide a child. You can limit the hiding places to one room. If you are entertaining only one child, you will have to be the "seeker," but at least you can rest and close your eyes while the hiding is going on. If other seekers are present, you can take it easy.

Hiding an object in plain sight Choose something small to hide — something like a safety pin, a walnut, or a button. The hider's art is to place the object in plain sight, but where it will blend with its background and not be easily detected — the safety pin on a slat of the Venetian blinds, the walnut in a dried-flower arrangement, the button in an ash tray. Small children are usually quicker finders in this game than adults, because their eyes are newer and sharper.

Hiding an object, either concealed or in full view, is a good game for two or three little ones who like the scene to change quickly. They are the actors, the movers, the doers. You can be the referee.

Hiding a clock Hiding an alarm clock with a fairly loud tick is fun. The hider can muffle the tick with a pillow or blanket, but he is not supposed to extinguish it entirely. Alert listening should lead to the place. If you want a little change from noisy, rambunctious children to quiet, listening ones, try hiding a clock.

Imaginary hiding This is a good one to play with a child whose activity must be limited. You say, "I hid my thimble in the kitchen. Where is it?" and Katy guesses until she says the right place. When the possibilities of the kitchen are exhausted, it is easy to move in imagination to another room — in Katy's house or in yours.

Where ARE you? Say in a singsong voice (with special emphasis on the word *are*), "Jerry, where *are* you?" Jerry answers in the same singsong way: "On a sailboat," "In an Eskimo's igloo," "In an elephant's eye." The wilder the answer, the more fun. Very small children may make literal answers like "Behind the door" or "In my bed," but they soon try to outdo one another in imagination. If only one child is present, this can be a game of one question and one moment, or it can be extended. More than likely, Jerry will want his turn to ask, "Where *are* you?" Then you can indulge your fancy with answers like: "Dancing through the Milky Way," or "On a safari in Africa," or "In a rocket ship on my way to Mars."

Variation: What are you DOING? When this is the question, Mary's answers can be "Flying my jet plane,"

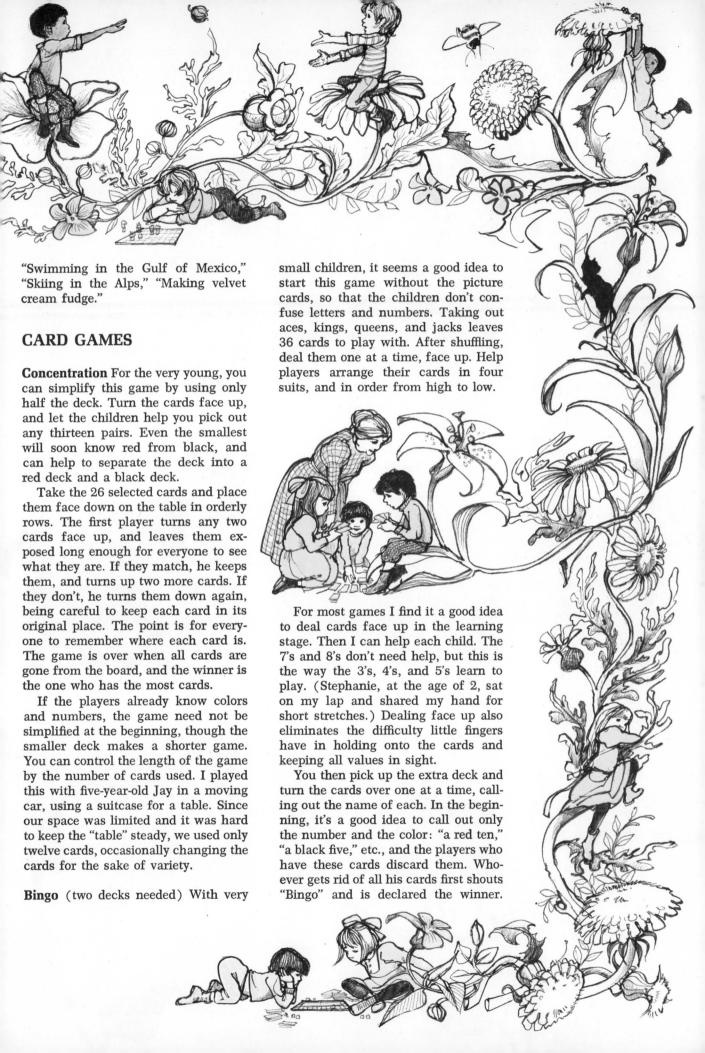

"Swimming in the Gulf of Mexico," "Skiing in the Alps," "Making velvet cream fudge."

CARD GAMES

Concentration For the very young, you can simplify this game by using only half the deck. Turn the cards face up, and let the children help you pick out any thirteen pairs. Even the smallest will soon know red from black, and can help to separate the deck into a red deck and a black deck.

Take the 26 selected cards and place them face down on the table in orderly rows. The first player turns any two cards face up, and leaves them exposed long enough for everyone to see what they are. If they match, he keeps them, and turns up two more cards. If they don't, he turns them down again, being careful to keep each card in its original place. The point is for everyone to remember where each card is. The game is over when all cards are gone from the board, and the winner is the one who has the most cards.

If the players already know colors and numbers, the game need not be simplified at the beginning, though the smaller deck makes a shorter game. You can control the length of the game by the number of cards used. I played this with five-year-old Jay in a moving car, using a suitcase for a table. Since our space was limited and it was hard to keep the "table" steady, we used only twelve cards, occasionally changing the cards for the sake of variety.

Bingo (two decks needed) With very

small children, it seems a good idea to start this game without the picture cards, so that the children don't confuse letters and numbers. Taking out aces, kings, queens, and jacks leaves 36 cards to play with. After shuffling, deal them one at a time, face up. Help players arrange their cards in four suits, and in order from high to low.

For most games I find it a good idea to deal cards face up in the learning stage. Then I can help each child. The 7's and 8's don't need help, but this is the way the 3's, 4's, and 5's learn to play. (Stephanie, at the age of 2, sat on my lap and shared my hand for short stretches.) Dealing face up also eliminates the difficulty little fingers have in holding onto the cards and keeping all values in sight.

You then pick up the extra deck and turn the cards over one at a time, calling out the name of each. In the beginning, it's a good idea to call out only the number and the color: "a red ten," "a black five," etc., and the players who have these cards discard them. Whoever gets rid of all his cards first shouts "Bingo" and is declared the winner.

You have to have eyes everywhere to see that players don't overlook opportunities, and this is where you can help to equalize abilities while children are learning. You can have a hand of your own if you like (and of course you *must* have if you are playing with only one child), but you will be so busy helping the other players that you will lose.

When the children know the numbers 2 to 10, it is time to play with the full deck and learn A for ace, K for king, Q for queen, and J for Jack. As the children learn, the game grows more sophisticated, and you now call out not "a red ten," but "the ten of hearts," not "a black nine," but "the nine of clubs." At this stage, children can conceal their hands if they prefer.

Pig or Donkey Choose from the deck as many sets of four as there are players. For example, if three are playing the deck can be four aces, four 2's, and four 9's (any three sets). If four are playing, another set of four must be added.

In this game, cards must be dealt face down, one at a time after they have been shuffled. Each player will have four cards. The point of the game is to get all four of any one rank in your hand. Players look at their cards and to begin the game, everyone discards one card, face down, to his left; and then picks up the card on his right and puts it in his hand. The play continues in this way, everyone discarding at the same time, and adding a new card to his hand. You can help with the timing, and children enjoy chanting together, "Put one down," and "Pick one up." As soon as any player gets four cards alike, he stops exchanging and quietly places his forefinger at the side of his nose. As quickly as each other player notices what has happened, he, too, stops playing and puts his finger beside his nose. The last to notice must say the letter "p" (and the scorekeeper writes "p" under that player's name). The second time he's last he takes the letter "i", and says "p-i" out loud and so on. Usually each player gets at least one letter. The first player to get "p-i-g—pig" is the loser and the game starts all over.

A variation on this game is Donkey. If four people are playing the game, pick three things to put in the center of the table (for example, three spoons — but don't use forks!). Always use one less item than there are players. When a player gets four cards alike, instead of putting his finger on the side of his nose, he quietly reaches for a spoon. As soon as the other players notice, they reach for spoons, too. The person caught without a spoon gets the letter "d". The first one to get "d-o-n-k-e-y—

donkey" is the loser. But since everyone almost always gets at least one letter (it's the very quick hand that doesn't!), the loser doesn't lose too badly.

Pig and Donkey can be played with any children old enough to *match* four numbers or four letters, whether they can read them or not. Stephanie enjoyed it when she was five. You can also help the smallest and if the same child becomes Pig or Donkey too often, you can tactfully switch to another game. In fact, children sometimes get along better at card playing if an adult plays with them. At other times, of course, they'd rather play alone. When in doubt, ask them! Or use your own good judgment.

Old Maid (part or all of one deck) If you are playing with only one child, it's a good idea to start with only part of a deck. Whatever cards are removed from the deck must be removed in pairs — for instance, all the picture cards except one queen. Whether a full deck or a partial deck is used, one queen stays in, and this is the Old Maid. Deal all cards, and give players time to sort them and discard any pairs they have. Then a player draws a card from the hand of his neighbor on the right (without looking, of course) and adds it to his hand. If it matches a card he already has, he discards the pair, and offers his hand to his left neighbor to choose. The player who has the queen is eager to get rid of it, and sometimes it changes hands several times before all the cards are paired off and one player is stuck with the Old Maid.

Fish (one deck) Shuffle cards and deal them one at a time. If two are playing, each player gets seven cards; if more are playing, five. The rest of the deck is placed face down in the middle of the table and becomes the "stock." The point is for the players to get books, that is, four cards of one rank.

The player to the left of the dealer begins by asking another player (any-

one he chooses) for cards that he needs. For instance, if he has two tens in his hand, he may say, "Mike, give me all your tens." If Mike has any tens, he must hand them over. If he has none, he says, "Fish," and the player must draw the top card from the stock. If the player should happen to draw a ten, or if he obtained what he asked for from Mike, his turn continues until he is unsuccessful in getting a desired card.

When a player gets four cards of one rank, he shows them to the others, and keeps the book on the table in front of him. The winner is the one with the most books at the end of the game.

Animals Before the play starts, each child decides what animal he will be. Long names like *rhinoceros* and *hippopotamus* are popular, because they make it difficult for opponents.

The whole deck is dealt, and each player leaves his hand face down in a neat pile in front of him. At each turn, a player turns up his top card and places it in front of his hand, making a trash pile. Whenever this card matches the exposed card on any other trash pile (two fives, two queens, etc.), the two players involved try to call out each other's animal name. Whoever can say the right name first gets the other player's trash pile. When a hand

is played out, the trash pile is turned over to become a hand again, as at the beginning.

This game is better for three or more players, because there is no trick to remembering just one animal. Some people play until one person gets all the cards, but I think it is more fun to end the game when one person loses all his cards, letting the others count their cards to determine the winner. This speeds things up, keeps everyone interested, and makes time for more games (and more winners).

If you want to make the game more difficult (and more hilarious), call out the *noise* the animal makes, instead of his name. In this case, familiar animals are used and the players must decide on the noise before the game begins — *bow-wow, meow, oink-oink, squeak-squeak,* etc.

Other games you may want to introduce to children

Slapjack
Forms of solitaire
Forms of rummy
I Doubt It

For more card games, see:
FIFTY CARD GAMES FOR CHILDREN.
Vernon Quinn. Whitman. 1946.

WORD GAMES

Words in a word (as soon as children can spell and write) This is for one child, or for two or more in competition. The players list smaller words they can make out of the letters of one large one — or better still, of the letters of two related words that have something to do with the season of the year. For instance:

Saint Valentine
George Washington
Easter morning
Independence Day
Halloween night
Christmas Eve

If children are competing, their skills are likely to be unequal, and you had better have an understanding at the beginning that you may help the youngest. The more unequal the abilities, the more quickly the less able players will tire of the game. After ten or fifteen minutes, you can suggest that the lists be put away for another day when the players can see if they are able to add more words. Or on the second round, players can give each other words. They may like to make up a scoring system where each one gets a point for each word the other didn't have.

If only one child is playing, he may want to keep on for quite a while. Save his list and give it back to him at a later date — when he will be surprised to find that he can add more words.

Words beginning with your initials Have children tell as many words as they can think of beginning with the initial of their first name. Older children may want to use two or even three initials, and if two with the same last name are competing they can choose a list of ten *things* beginning with their last initial, and then make separate lists. Help them choose the list of things, or give them a picture dictionary. Thus, the Raders children may agree on *roses, rabbits, rings, rain, rats, robins, ribs, reasons, rakes,* and *roads.* Margaret Lynn Raders comes up with a list like *many little roses, more lively rabbits, my lovely rings, much less rain, mean lazy rats,* while Laura Ann Raders is writing *little adorable robins, long animal ribs, least agreeable reasons, lopsided antique rakes, level American roads.* This is a good time-filler when you have to wait for something to happen.

Opposites Here is another diversion for odd minutes. You briefly explain the game, and then say, "Up," and Mike responds, "Down." If Mike is only three, you can remain the leader throughout the game, simply calling out as many words as you can think of that have opposites; but as he gets older Mike will want a turn to call, too, and he will say, "Big," and wait for your response, "Little."

Rocket (the old homonym game of *Teakettle*) There are several ways to play this game, depending on the skill of the children. One way is for you (the adult) to take most of the responsibility. You make a sentence like the following: "In the woods I saw a big black ROCKET, and he had ROCKET feet." Explain to the children that they are to name the word that could fill both blanks. They will soon say *bear* (*bare*), and you can explain as much or as little as you like about the spelling (depending on the age of the children). After you have given them an example or two, children will want to make up the sentences and let you guess.

Or you can make it a writing game. Write one form of the homonym at the left side of the page, and let the players write other forms and make up sentences. Your list might begin with *two, four, inn, brake, meet, beet, here, dear, ate,* and *maid.* As children learn more words, they will also learn more homonyms, and the game can get more difficult as the players' skills increase.

"I love my love with an A" The first player says, "I love my love with an A, because he is *affectionate.* His name is *Al,* and I sent him to *Alabama* to get me some *apples.*" The next player goes on, "I love my love with a B, because she is *beautiful.* Her name is *Beth,* and I sent her to *Boston* to get me some *beans.*" Once through the alphabet is enough.

This is the kind of game adults like children to play, because there are no losers. There is just the fun of playing. Even a child who isn't sure of the alphabet can play "I love my love with an A" with an occasional assist. The game is a help in learning beginning sounds as well as A-B-C's. You can keep the game moving, but don't help more than necessary. You have probably heard a little one say, "Don't tell me. Let me think of my own word."

Time for a rhyme This is another game that can be simple or complex. In the simple form, you say a word that has many rhymes (like man), and ask Johnny and Mary how many rhyming words they can think of — *can, fan, began, ran,* etc. When they know the alphabet, they can run through it

mentally to see if they have overlooked any rhyming words.

Let them take turns in naming the word for which rhymes are to be found — but steer them away from words like *orange* and *silver,* which have no rhymes. (A thoughtful child will not take your word for this, but may spend a long time trying to think up a rhyme nobody else knows!)

When the children have developed facility with rhymes, a more difficult variety can be introduced: The player has to ask a question which can be answered with two rhyming words. For instance:

What is a fat hog?
A big pig.

What is a light brown skillet?
A tan pan.

What is a person with auburn hair?
A red head.

What is a beautiful town?
A pretty city.

What is a dog's bark?
Bow-wow.

This variation is not easy, but it is interesting. Not only do the players have to think up two rhyming words that make sense together, but they also have to make a good question that will not give everything away by using one of the rhyming words. You can play it while something else is going on — You can be starting dinner and your Beth and Carl can be building or coloring or drawing, when one or the other may announce: "Time for a Rhyme! What does a 150-watt electric bulb make?" (Answer: A bright light.)

Categories Since a child's own name is endlessly interesting to him, this is a good way to introduce the game of *Categories.*

Print the name at the top of the page and several categories down the side:

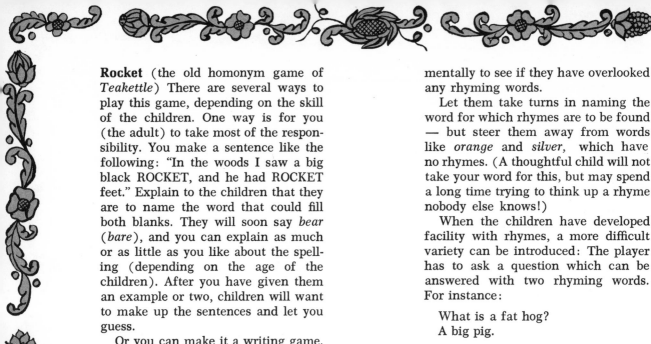

	A	L	I	S	O	N
PLANT	ASH		IVY	SUMAC		
FOOD		LEMON				NUTS
PLACE	ATLANTA				OREGON	
NAME				SHARON		NEAL
ANIMAL		LION	IBEX			

If Alison is coming to see you, you can prepare the game ahead of time, and give her a long time to fill in the blanks. Or send her the game in a letter, with a few blanks filled in and the rest for her to do.

PROVERBS

Whether or not we hear proverbs quoted very often, they are part of our heritage. A list of some that are well-known follows, and you can make your own additions. See how many games you can make up that use proverbs. Here are a few suggestions:

A writing game (for one child, or for two or more in competition)

Choose ten proverbs. Scramble the words. (For instance, "A day away doctor keeps an the apple.") Write the ten scrambled proverbs on a sheet of paper, and save it for a convalescent child, or for a quiet time for a healthy child.

An acting game (for one child or for several)

Read a list of proverbs, or have the children read them to you. Let each one choose three or four that he would like to act. Children take turns acting out proverbs while others guess. Sometimes two children working together can do a better job.

VARIATION If you are entertaining only one child, you can discuss a proverb with him and see if he can think of more than one way to act it out. This is a chance to talk about what a proverb really means.

Proverb stories (Violet Eder told me about playing this with her granddaughter Margaret.)

Make a list of proverbs. Give everyone a little time to study the list; then take turns telling an anecdote that illustrates a proverb, and see who is first to guess the right proverb. (For instance: A mother calls out to her little boy, "You've ripped your jeans. Come in and let me mend them, or I'll have a bigger job tomorrow." Proverb: A stitch in time saves nine.)

A remembering game Each player in turn says a proverb until he can't remember any more. Each one keeps his own score (one point for each proverb), or an adult keeps score for all. Set a time limit.

Some proverbs

A bird in the hand is worth two in the bush.
A friend in need is a friend indeed.
A leopard can't change his spots.
All things come to him who waits.
All work and no play makes Jack a dull boy.
An apple a day keeps the doctor away.
A new broom sweeps clean.

A penny saved is a penny earned.
A place for everything
and everything in its place.
As busy as a bee.
A soft answer turns away wrath.
A stitch in time saves nine.
A watched pot never boils.
Beggars can't be choosers.
Better late than never.
Birds of a feather flock together.
Don't count your chickens
before they are hatched.
Don't cry over spilt milk.
Don't make a mountain out of a molehill.
Don't put all your eggs in one basket.

Don't put off till tomorrow what you can do today.
Early to bed and early to rise
makes a man healthy and wealthy and wise.
God helps those who help themselves.
Great oaks from little acorns grow.
Handsome is as handsome does.
Haste makes waste.
Home is where the heart is.
If at first you don't succeed,
try, try again.
It takes two to make a quarrel.
Little pitchers have big ears.
Love me, love my dog.
Out of the frying pan into the fire.
Paddle your own canoe.
People who live in glass houses shouldn't throw stones.
Red sky in the morning,
Sailor take warning.
Red sky at night.
Sailor's delight.

Seeing is believing.
Shoe the horse and shoe the mare,
But let the little colt go bare.
The early bird catches the worm.
The way to a man's heart
is through his stomach.
Too many cooks spoil the broth.
Two heads are better than one.
Two's company, three's a crowd.
Two wrongs do not make a right.
Turn about's fair play.
You can catch more flies with honey than with vinegar.
You can lead a horse to water,
but you can't make him drink.
You can't eat your cake and have it.
You can't teach an old dog new tricks.

GUESSING GAMES

I Spy (with colors or letters or sounds) Our friends, the Woodwards, knew this game as "Twit, Twit, Twee, What Do I See?" If you are playing with very young children who are just learning colors, make the game *obvious*. That is, look straight at the sky, and say, "I Spy something blue." But with a more knowledgeable child, you make it a

point *not* to look at the object you "spy." Players who know their colors like to play this in a car, because the object "spied" goes out of range so quickly that the guessers are left in the dark. After giving up, they find out the "something orange" was a glass of orange juice on a billboard a mile back.

In playing with initial letters, either the name or the sound of the letter can be given. Children who don't know letters can use the sound: For *book* they can say, "I Spy something that begins with *buh*," while the others say "something that begins with B."

Variation: I'm Thinking of Something (with either colors or beginning sounds) is a more imaginative version of *I Spy*, and the sky is the limit. It's a good travel game, or one to quiet children down at bedtime. When I was a little girl, my brothers and I used to play something like this while we were taking an afternoon rest. We called it "Seeing things in the ceiling," but in our version the guessing was eliminated. We just closed our eyes and took turns describing what we "saw" — each one trying to outdo the others with things like "a chocolate ice cream soda as big as this house," or "the Easter bunny with a hundred baskets filled with candy."

How Much or How Many? Put straight pins in a see-through plastic box or pill bottle, beans or buttons in a jar, and let children guess how many there are. If there is more than one child, write down the guesses, and then let them pour out the contents and count to see which one came closest. You can hold up a quart bottle partly filled with water ("Guess how many ounces"), a length of string ("Guess how many inches"), or a book ("Guess how many pages").

Ask your Margie or Pat or Sherry if she can think up more things to make "How Much or How Many?" guesses about.

Feel bag Into a paper bag, put small objects (a spool of thread, a bottle cap, a penny, a rubber jar ring, a thimble, a pencil — or things with different textures, such as a piece of sandpaper, a scrap of velvet, a feather, a marshmallow, an orange), after showing them to the children. Let each one reach into the bag, in turn, pick out one object, and name it before he pulls it out to see if he has named it correctly.

Smell bag This is like the preceding game, except that you choose things with a decided aroma — an onion, a clove of garlic, a sachet, an apple, etc. — and let children smell each one before the game begins. In this case, you put only one thing in the bag at a time. Then the child, with his eyes tight shut, sniffs the bag and gives his verdict.

Remember that you aren't trying to mystify the children. You're helping them increase their sensory perception!

Drop It This time we think of *sound*. Stand behind a kitchen counter (or anything that conceals what you are doing). Drop something. You can use a pot lid, a book, a cardboard box, a plastic bottle, a potato, a tin can — all of which the players should see before the game begins.

Children listen to the sound and see who can be first to identify what you dropped. If you are playing with only one child, he keeps on till he guesses correctly.

SPECIAL GAMES

Anita Vance learned the two ancient games that follow from her grandmother more than half a century ago.

Knock It Off, Pinch It Off, or Take It Off If you want to divert one or two children (or even one child) from an unhappy mood, sit down, double your left hand into a fist, place it on your left knee with the thumb sticking up, and announce, "Knock it off, pinch it off, or take it off." This is the signal for the children to build up on your fist with theirs, each one sticking up his thumb for the next one to grasp. You then ask each one in turn, "Knock it off, pinch it off, or take it off?" and he says which action he prefers. If it is "Knock it off," knock off the little fist with a glancing blow from the side. For "Pinch it off," squeeze from below; and for "Take it off," lift from above.

Children are interested in one another's choices, and if you are playing with only one, he will probably suggest a different action for each of his fists.

Variation:

When the fists are disposed of, and you still have the children's attention, say, "I'm hiding behind the old

church door and I've got the key! The first one that smiles or shows his teeth must stand on his head" (or run to the front door and back, or drink a glass of water backward* — or any action that will be fun for the child to do.)

This goes on as long as children are interested. There is no real connection between the two parts described above, but after children have played the first part a time or two, they know what to expect.

William Trembletoe

Count out with this old rhyme:

William Trembletoe, he's a good fisherman.
Catches fishes, puts them in dishes.
Catches hens, puts them in pens.
Some lay eggs, some lay none.
Wire, briar, limberlock,
Three geese in a flock.
One flew east and one flew west,
And one flew over the cuckoo's nest.
O-U-T spells out.
You old dirty dishrag.
You get out.

The one who is OUT goes to another room, and the others decide in what character he is to come back: "Come back like an elephant," "Come back like a snake," "Come back like a galloping horse," etc.

* To drink a glass of water backward, you lean over the sink and drink from the back of the glass. When I was a little girl, we considered this a cure for hiccups—perhaps because it makes it necessary to take small sips.

If only one child is present, it is surprising how many times an adult can make the counting-out rhyme come out right (that is, so that the child takes the active part). With more than one child the adult can see that all children get turns by starting the counting-out rhyme with a different child each time.

Command If your companion is restive and needs action at a time when *you* need quiet, you can suggest, "Let's play *Command*." Then you say, "Jay, I *command* you to bring me something soft" (or hard, smooth, fuzzy, cold, green, heavy, etc.). When all children present have had a turn, then you say, "Jay, I *command* you to take this soft thing back where it came from," and so on for each child until everything is back in place.

Hull Gull Lee and Merle Woodward introduced this game to me, and then I found out my husband had played it as a boy. I thought it was indigenous to Texas — until I learned it goes back to ancient Greece!

Use beans or corn or buttons or anything small enough to be held in the hand in quantity. Give each player ten. (Later they can play with 15 or 20, or even more, if they wish.) The first player hides a few of his beans in his hand and announces that he is ready to play by saying: *Hull Gull.*

Second: "Handful?"

First: "How many?"

The second guesses. If he guesses the right number, he gets his opponent's beans. If he guesses wrong, he gives up the difference between his guess and the right number. That is, if the first player is holding five, and the second guesses either three or seven, he gives up two beans.

Then the second player hides an unknown number in his hand, and it is then the first player's turn to guess. And so the game goes until one player gets all the beans.

Giraffe (good for a few minutes of peace and quiet) When things get too noisy, say, "Let's play *Giraffe*. A giraffe can't make a sound, so everyone must be quiet." The first one to speak will tease others into speaking, and the one who holds out the longest is the Prize Giraffe.

For more games, see:
THE COMPLETE BOOK OF GAMES.
Clement Wood and Gloria Goddard.
Doubleday. 1940.
A TREASURY OF GAMES.
Carl Withers. Grosset & Dunlap. 1964.

Songs, Rhymes, Riddles, and Finger Plays

Singing to — and with — children is one of the most enjoyable pastimes imaginable. Babies who are sung to are more likely to become people who like to sing, and music has a way of uniting a group in enjoyment. My mother and father sang an assortment of songs and we children loved them.

Here is a sampling of old songs, rhymes, riddles, and finger plays. But who was it who said, "A folk song is a song that everybody else sings the wrong version of"? The same could be said about old rhymes and tales.

Here you will find *my* favorites. They will remind you of your own. If you knew "Fox went forth one moonshiny night" as "Fox went out on a chilly night," go ahead and sing it your way.

Looby Loo

1. Here we go Looby Loo, here we go Looby Light,
   Here we go Looby Loo all on a Saturday night.
   I put my right hand in, I put my right hand out,
   I give my right hand a shake, shake, shake,
   And turn myself about.

2. Refrain (first two lines above)
   Repeat above with *left hand* in place of *right hand*.

3. Right foot

4. Left foot

5. Whole self

   It is fun to sing this with a pre-school child and help him learn the difference between *right* and *left*.

   "Looby Loo" and the song that follows will be learned as circle games when children go "out into the world," but one child alone (or with the family) can have fun with them, too.

61

Did You Ever See a Lassie?

Did you ever see a lassie, a lassie, a lassie, (or laddie)
Did you ever see a lassie go this way and that?
Go this way, go that way, go this way, go that way,
Did you ever see a lassie go this way and that?

This is a lovely song for the very young. "This way" and "that way" may be any gesture you want to suggest to the child — or that he suggests to you.

She'll Be Comin' Round the Mountain

1. She'll be comin' round the mountain when she comes,
   She'll be comin' round the mountain when she comes,
   She'll be comin' round the mountain, she'll be comin round the mountain,
   She'll be comin' round the mountain when she comes.

2. She'll be drivin' six white horses when she comes,
   She'll be drivin' six white horses when she comes,
   She'll be drivin' six white horses, she'll be drivin' six white horses,
   She'll be drivin' six white horses when she comes. Whoa back!
   (While saying "Whoa Back!" pull on imaginary reins)

3. Oh, we'll all go down to meet her when she comes. . . .
   (Make wolf whistle and roll eyes)

4. Oh, we'll kill the old red rooster when she comes . . . Hack! Hack!
   (Spoken while making chopping motions)

5. Oh, we'll all have chicken an' dumplin's when she comes . . .
   Yum! Yum!
   (Spoken while rubbing stomach)

6. Oh, she'll have to wash the dishes when she comes . . . Crash! Bang!
   (Spoken while placing hands over ears)

Frog Went Courting

Frog went courting, he did ride. A-hmm.
Frog went courting, he did ride,
Sword and pistol by his side. A-hmm.

First he came to Miss Mousie's den. A-hmm.
First he came to Miss Mousie's den.
Said he, "Missie Mouse, will you let me in?" A-hmm.

"Oh yes, kind sir, I'll sit and spin." A-hmm.
"Oh yes, kind sir, I'll sit and spin.
Just lift the latch and walk right in." A-hmm.

He took Miss Mousie upon his knee. A-hmm.
He took Miss Mousie upon his knee.
Said he, "Missie Mouse, will you marry me?" A-hmm.

"Not without Uncle Rat's consent," A-hmm.
"Not without Uncle Rat's consent
Would I marry the President." A-hmm.

6. Uncle Rat he grinned and smiled. A-hmm.
   Uncle Rat he grinned and smiled
   To see his niece such a silly child. A-hmm.

7. Where shall the wedding supper be? A-hmm.
   Where shall the wedding supper be?
   Down in yonder hollow tree. A-hmm.

8. What shall we have for the bride to eat? A-hmm.
   What shall we have for the bride to eat?
   A piece of bread and a piece of meat. A-hmm.

9. They all went sailing out on the lake. A-hmm.
   They all went sailing out on the lake,
   And got swallowed up by a big black snake. A-hmm.

10. Bottles and glasses upon the shelf. A-hmm.
    Bottles and glasses upon the shelf.
    If you want any more, you can sing it yourself. A-hmm.

(Accent on A—short *A* as in *cat*.
This is the way Grandma Graham sang it in Pittsburgh, Pa.)

If you learned this song a different way, sing it your way.

Nick Nack Paddy Wack

1. This old man, he played one,
   He played Nick Nack just for fun,
   With a Nick Nack Paddy Wack, give the dog a bone,
   This old man came rolling home.

2. This old man, he played two,
   He played Nick Nack on my shoe,
   With a Nick Nack, etc.

3. This old man, he played three,
   He played Nick Nack up a tree, etc.

4. This old man, he played four,
   He played Nick Nack on the door, etc.

5. This old man, he played five,
   He played Nick Nack on the drive, etc.

6. This old man, he played six,
   He played Nick Nack with some sticks, etc.

7. This old man, he played seven,
   He played Nick Nack up to heaven, etc.

8. This old man, he played eight,
   He played Nick Nack on my gate, etc.

9. This old man, he played nine,
   He played Nick Nack down the line, etc.

10. This old man, he played ten,
    He played Nick Nack now and then, etc.

64

Fox Went Forth One Moonshiny Night

1. Fox went forth one moonshiny night,
   Prayed for the moon to give him light.
   He'd many miles to travel that night
   Before he reached the town-O, the town-O, the town-O.
   He'd many miles to travel that night
   Before he reached the town-O.

2. First he came to the farmer's yard,
   Ducks and geese were all a-feared.
   The best of you shall grease my beard
   Before I leave the town-O, the town-O, the town-O.
   The best of you (repeat as in stanza 1)

3. Grabbed the old black duck by the neck,
   Flung her over across his back,
   Made the old duck go quack, quack, quack!
   And her legs hung dangling down-O, down-O, down-O.
   Made the old duck, etc.

4. Carried her home unto his den
   Where he had young ones nine or ten,
   Carved her up without knife or fork,
   And the young ones picked the bones-O, the bones-O, the bones-O.
   Carved her up, etc.

5. Old Mother Wibble-Wobble jumped out of bed.
   Out the window stuck her head,
   "John, John, John! The black duck's gone!
   The fox ran through the town-O, the town-O, the town-O!
   John, John, John! etc."

Maybe you know this as "Fox Went Out on a Chilly Night."

There's a Hole in the Bucket

1. There's a hole in the bucket, dear Liza, dear Liza,
   There's a hole in the bucket, dear Liza, a hole.

2. Then mend it, dear Georgie, dear Georgie, dear Georgie,
   Then mend it, dear Georgie, dear Georgie, mend it.

3. With what shall I mend it, dear Liza, . . . with what?

4. With a straw, dear Georgie, . . . a straw.

5. The straw is too long, dear Liza, . . . too long.

6. Then cut it, dear Georgie, . . . cut it.

7. With what shall I cut it, dear Liza, . . . with what?

8. With a knife, dear Georgie, . . . a knife.

9. The knife is too dull, dear Liza, . . . too dull.

10. Then sharpen it, dear Georgie, . . . sharpen it.

11. With what shall I sharpen it, dear Liza, . . . with what?

12. With a stone, dear Georgie, . . . a stone.

13. The stone is too dry, dear Liza, . . . too dry.

14. Then wet it, dear Georgie, . . . wet it.

15. With what shall I wet it, dear Liza, . . . with what?

16. With water, dear Georgie, . . . with water.

17. In what shall I get it, dear Liza, . . . in what?

18. In a bucket, dear Georgie, . . . in a bucket.

19. There's a hole in the bucket, dear Liza, . . . a hole.

Lazy Mary

1. Lazy Mary, will you get up, will you get up, will you get up?
   Lazy Mary, will you get up, will you get up today?

2. What will you give me if I get up, if I get up, if I get up?
   What will you give me if I get up, if I get up today?
   (Spoken) A glass of milk and a cookie. (Or let children make up answers, varying the things to eat.)

3. No, Mother, I won't get up, I won't get up, I won't get up,
   No, Mother, I won't get up, I won't get up today.

4. Lazy Mary, will you get up, will you get up, will you get up?
   Lazy Mary, will you get up, will you get up today?

5. Same as 2 (above)
   (Spoken) A nice young man with rosy cheeks.

6. Yes, Mother, I will get up, I will get up, I will get up.
   Yes, Mother, I will get up, I will get up today.

John Brown's Baby

John Brown's baby had a cold upon its chest,
John Brown's baby had a cold upon its chest,
John Brown's baby had a cold upon its chest,
And they rubbed it with camphorated oil.

Children enjoy singing this with gestures. First sing through the song as it is written. The second time omit the word *baby* and fold arms as if cradling a baby. Each time omit one more word, as follows:

3. Omit *cold.* (Give a short cough.)

4. Omit *chest.* (Point to chest.)

5. Omit *rubbed it.* (Make rubbing motion on chest.)

6. Omit *camphorated oil.* (Sniff.)

7. Sing through as in the beginning, with all the words.

Three Little Pigs Lay Under a Gate

1. Three little pigs lay under a gate, gate, gate,
   She-ate, she-ate, (Snort)* She-I-diddle-date.
   Lillie-bu-lerro, lillie-bu-lerro, lillie-bu-lerro, lillie-bu-lerro,
   Father's a bonny wee man, man, man,
   She-ann, she-ann, (Snort)* She-I-diddle-dan!
   Oh! Father's a bonny wee man.

2. Three little pigs, they lay upon straw, straw, straw,
   She-aw, she-aw, (Snort)* She-I-diddle-daw.
   Lillie-bu-lerro, lillie-bu-lerro, lillie-bu-lerro, lillie-bu-lerro,
   Father's a bonny wee man, man, man,
   She-ann, she-ann, (Snort)* She-I-diddle-dan!
   Oh! Father's a bonny wee man.

* Draw the breath into the back of the throat like a snore.

Go Tell Aunt Rhody

Go tell Aunt Rhody, go tell Aunt Rhody,
Go tell Aunt Rhody her old gray goose is dead —
The one she was saving, the one she was saving,
The one she was saving to make a feather bed.

Make a list of songs you know that children would like.
Teach them when you get a chance.

Do you remember these?

Farmer in the Dell
Do You Know the Muffin Man?
Oats, Peas, Beans, and Barley
   Grow
Here We Go Round the Mulberry
   Bush
London Bridge
Go In and Out the Window
Skip to My Lou
Way Down Yonder in the
   Paw-Paw Patch

Blood on the Saddle
The Bear Went Over the
   Mountain
Old MacDonald Had a Farm
I Went to the Animal Fair
The Green Grass Grows All
   Around
Billy Boy
Michael, Row the Boat Ashore

Sources of other songs:
THE AMERICAN SONGBAG. *Carl Sandburg. Harcourt. 1927.*
THE FOLK SONGS OF NORTH AMERICA. *Alan Lomax. Doubleday. 1966.*
FIRESIDE BOOK OF FOLK SONGS. *Margaret Bradford Boni and Norman Lloyd.*
                              Simon & Schuster. 1947.
THE BEST SINGING GAMES. *Edgar S. Bley. Sterling. 1957.*

OLD RHYMES

These are rhymes I remember from my childhood. Write down the ones *you* remember, and ask your children if they are still saying them.

I can wash the dishes,
I can sweep the floor.
I can kiss the nicest boy
Behind the parlor door.

First he gave me peaches,
Then he gave me pears,
Then he gave me fifty cents,
Kissed me on the stairs.

Gave him back his peaches,
Gave him back his pears,
Gave him back his fifty cents,
Kicked him down the stairs.

(The above was sung to a tune played on the black keys of the piano, and every little girl seemed to know it.)

Mother, Mother I am sick.
Send for the doctor quick, quick, quick.
Doctor, doctor, shall I die?
Yes, my dear, but don't you cry.
How many carriages shall I have?
1, 2, 3 (Count until jumper misses.)

Salt, vinegar, mustard, pepper,
Cedar, cider, red hot PEPPER.

(The rope turned faster on the second line.)

For counting out

Ibbity, bibbity, sibbity, sab,
Ibbity, bibbity, canal boat,
Dictionary down the ferry,
Out goes Y-O-U.

Acka-backa-soda cracker,
Acka-backa-boo.
In comes Uncle Sam.
Out goes YOU.

For jumping rope

To let, to let,
Inquire within.
When I move out
(*Name of another child*) moves in.

For bouncing ball

One, two, buckle my shoe.
Three, four, shut the door.
Five, six, pick up sticks.
Seven, eight, lay them straight.
Nine, ten, a big fat hen.
Eleven, twelve, we will delve.
Thirteen, fourteen, maids a-courting.
Fifteen, sixteen, maids a-kissing.
Seventeen, eighteen, maids a-waiting.
Nineteen, twenty, my plate's empty.

Naught, one, the work is done.
Two, three, the jubilee.

Four, five, ducks are alive.
Six, seven, stars in heaven.
Eight, nine, Queen, Queen Caroline
Washed her face in turpentine.
Turpentine made it shine,
Queen, Queen Caroline.

One, two, three, O'Leary,
I saw Mrs. Cheery
Sitting on a bumble-eerie,
Eating chocolate sodas.

OTHER OLD RHYMES

Engine, engine, number nine,
Riding on Chicago line.
When she's polished won't she shine!
Engine, engine, number nine.

One, two, three, four, five,
I caught a hare alive.
Six, seven, eight, nine, ten,
I let him go again.
Why did I let him go?
Because he bit my finger so.

Old Dan Tucker was a fine old man,
Washed his face in a frying pan,
Combed his hair with a steamboat wheel,
And died with a toothache in his heel.

Little Sally Ann,
Sitting in the sand,
Weeping and crying for a young man!
Rise, Sally, rise,
Wipe your weeping eyes.
Turn to the east and
Turn to the west,
And turn to the one
That you love best.

Did you eever, Iver, over
In your leefy, lifey, lofe
See the deevil, dievil, dovel
Kiss his weefy,
                    wifey,
                            wofe?

No, I neever, niver, nover
In my leefy, lifey, lofe
Saw the deevil, dievil, dovel
Kiss his weefy,
                    wifey,
                            wofe.

Susie Mariar

This is the story of Susie Mariar.
It started one night as she sat by the fire.
The fire was so hot, she jumped in a pot.
The pot was so black, she jumped in a crack.
The crack was so narrow,
   she jumped in a wheelbarrow.
The wheelbarrow was so low,
   she fell in the snow.
The snow was so white,
   she stayed there all night.
The night was so long, she sang a song.
The song was so sweet, she ran down the street.
The street was so clean, she picked up a bean.
The bean was so hard, she dropped it in lard.
The lard was so greasy, she jumped clean fleezy.
And when she came down,
   she ran through the town.
The town was so big, she jumped on a pig.
The pig jumped so high, she hit the sky.
She hit the sky and couldn't go higher,
But oh, what a ride had Susie Mariar!

See how many rhymes you can remember that begin "There was an old woman . . ."

Poor Old Lady, She's Going to Die

Poor old lady, she's going to die.
She swallowed a fly.
I don't know *why* she swallowed a fly.
Poor old lady, she's going to die.

Poor old lady, she's going to die.
She swallowed a spider
Way down inside 'er.
She swallowed the spider to catch the fly.
I don't know *why* she swallowed the fly.
Poor old lady, she's going to die.

Poor old lady, she's going to die.
She swallowed a bird.
How absurd, she swallowed a bird.
She swallowed the bird to catch the spider
That went b-r-r-mp way down inside 'er.
She swallowed the spider to catch the fly.
I don't know *why* she swallowed the fly.
Poor old lady, she's going to die.

Poor old lady, she's going to die.
She swallowed a cat.
Think of that, she swallowed a cat.
She swallowed the cat to catch the bird.
How absurd, she swallowed a bird.
She swallowed the bird to catch the spider
That went b-r-r-mp way down inside 'er.
She swallowed the spider to catch the fly.
I don't know *why* she swallowed the fly.
Poor old lady, she's going to die.

Poor old lady, she's going to die.
She swallowed a dog.
She swallowed a dog. She did—whole hog!—
She swallowed the dog to catch the cat.
(Finish as in preceding stanzas.)

Poor old lady, she's going to die.
She swallowed a cow.
I don't know *how* she swallowed a cow.
She swallowed the cow to catch the dog.
(Finish as above.)

Poor old lady, she's going to die.
She swallowed a horse.
She's dead, of course.

You may have heard this sung as a folk song, with somewhat different words, but I learned it first as a rhyme.

Mister Rabbit

Mister Rabbit, Mister Rabbit,
Your ears mighty long.
Yes, my Lord,
They're put on wrong.
Every little soul must shine, shine,
Every little soul must shine, shine, shine.

Mister Rabbit, Mister Rabbit,
Your foot's mighty red.
Yes, my Lord,
And I'm almost dead.
Every little soul must shine, shine,
Every little soul . . . etc.

Mister Rabbit, Mister Rabbit,
Your coat's mighty grey.
Yes, my Lord,
It was made that way.
Every little soul . . . etc.

Mister Rabbit, Mister Rabbit,
You're gettin' in the habit
Of goin' in my garden
An' eatin' up my cabbage.
Yes, my Lord,
My appetite is savage!
Every little soul . . . etc.

Mister Rabbit, Mister Rabbit,
Your tail's mighty white.
Yes, my Lord,
And I'm gettin' out of sight.
Every little soul must shine, shine,
Every little soul must shine, shine, shine.

To My Valentine

If apples were pears,
And peaches were plums,
And the rose had a different name;
If tigers were bears,
And fingers were thumbs,
I'd love you just the same!

Pumpkin Pie

P double inkin,
P double I,
P double unkin,
Pumpkin pie!

This Is the Key

This is the Key of the Kingdom.
In that Kingdom is a city;
In that city is a town;
In that town there is a street;
In that street there winds a lane;
In that lane there is a yard;
In that yard there is a house;
In that house there waits a room;
In that room an empty bed;
And on that bed a basket—
A Basket of Sweet Flowers,
    Of Flowers, of Flowers,
    A Basket of Sweet Flowers.

Flowers in a Basket;
Basket on the bed;
Bed in the chamber;
Chamber in the house;
House in the weedy yard;
Yard in the winding lane;
Lane in the broad street;
Street in the high town;
Town in the city;
City in the Kingdom—
This is the Key of the Kingdom;
Of the Kingdom this is the Key.

The Christmas Pudding

Into the basin put the plums,
    Stirabout, stirabout, stirabout!
Next the good white flour comes,
    Stirabout, stirabout, stirabout!

Sugar and peel and eggs and spice,
    Stirabout, stirabout, stirabout!
Mix them and fix them and cook them twice,
    Stirabout, stirabout, stirabout!

OLD RIDDLE RHYMES

Round as an apple,
Deep as a cup.
All the king's horses
Can't dig it up.
      (A well)

I have a little sister;
Her name is Peep-Peep.
She wades through the water
Deep, deep, deep.
She climbs the mountain
High, high, high.
Poor little thing!
She has only one eye.
      (A star)

Little Nancy Etticoat
In a white petticoat,
The longer she stands
The shorter she grows.
      (A candle)

A man without eyes
Saw plums on a tree.
He neither took plums, nor left plums.
Pray, how can that be?
   (Answer: A *one*-eyed man saw two
plums on a tree. He took *one* and left
one.)

Thirty white horses upon a red hill;
Now they tramp, now they champ,
now they stand still.
    [Teeth]

Two legs sat upon three legs
With one leg in his lap.
In comes four legs
And runs away with one leg.
Up jumps two legs,
Picks up three legs,
Throws it after four legs,
And makes him bring one leg back.

   (Answer: A man sits on a three-legged stool,
eating a leg of lamb. In comes a dog —
and the rest you can figure out.)

As I was going to St. Ives,
I met a man with seven wives.
Each wife had seven sacks;
Each sack had seven cats;
Each cat had seven kittens.
Kits, cats, sacks, and wives,
How many were going to St. Ives?

   (Answer: One. [The rest were
coming from there.])

RIDDLES

Make a little book of riddles to give to someone who likes them. This can be a little homemade book (see page 32) or a small looseleaf notebook that allows for additions. Here are some for a starter:

What do you call a bull when he is asleep?
A bulldozer.

What is the difference between the north shore of Long Island and the south shore of Long Island?
   On the north shore you see the Sound, and on the south shore you hear the sea.

Why is a giraffe's neck so long?
   Because his head is so far from his body.

What is a ten-letter word that starts with g-a-s?
Automobile.

What is gray, has four legs, and a trunk?
A mouse going on a vacation.

How can you make a blouse last?
Make the skirt first.

What animal has two humps and is found at the North Pole?
A lost camel.

Why did the little boy put suntan lotion on his chicken?
Because he liked dark meat.

What happens to a duck when he flies upside down?
He quacks up.

How does a witch tell time?
She wears a witch watch.

What has a foot on each side and a foot in the middle?
A yardstick.

What does "illegal" mean?
A sick bird.

How do you catch a squirrel?
Climb a tree and act like a nut.

What did the little boy say when his mother asked him if he had taken a bath?
"Is there one missing?"

Why do they measure the speed of ships in knots?
To keep the ocean tide.

Why did the little girl go outside with her purse open?
Because she heard there was going to be some change in the weather.

How do you keep a skunk from smelling?
Hold his nose.

What is a caterpillar?
A worm in a fur coat.

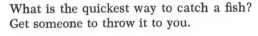

What is the quickest way to catch a fish?
Get someone to throw it to you.

Why isn't your hand 12-inches long?
Because then it would be a foot.

Why did the man mop up his spilled coffee with a piece of cake?
Because it was sponge cake.

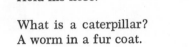

What did the mother ghost say to the baby ghost?
You must learn to spook when spooken to.

Why are the Middle Ages called the Dark Ages?
Because it was Knight time.

What is the tallest building in any city?
The public library, because it has the most stories.

Why is it cold in a football stadium?
Because there are so many fans.

What has arms and legs but no head?
A chair.

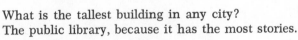

What has eight legs, three heads, six eyes, and two wings?
A man on a horse, carrying a parakeet.

What has one horn and gives milk?
A milk truck.

Why was the little girl afraid of a comb?
Because of its teeth.

Why does a rabbit have a shiny nose?
Because its powder puff is at the other end.

Why are fish smarter than insects?
Because they live in schools.

How can you divide seven apples among three people?
Make applesauce.

Why does Uncle Sam wear red, white, and blue suspenders?
To hold up his trousers.

How does a dog make friends?
He wags his tail instead of his tongue.

What room has no floor or ceiling or windows or doors?
A mushroom.

Why did the little boy take hay to bed with him?
To feed his nightmare.

Why did the little girl tiptoe past the medicine chest?
She didn't want to wake up the sleeping pills.

If you were locked in a room with nothing but a baseball and a bat, how would you get out?
Three strikes and you're out.

Sometimes old riddles turn up with new answers, like: What's black and white and red all over? Old answer: A newspaper. New answer: A sunburned zebra.
Why did the chicken cross the road? Old answer: To get to the other side. New answer: To see a man lay bricks.
Do you know other old riddles that have new answers?

TONGUE TWISTERS

Betty Botta (taught to me by Alice North, who learned it more than seventy years ago)

Betty Botta bought some butter.
"Now," said she, "this butter's bitter.
If I put it in my batter,
It will make the batter bitter."
So she bought a bit of butter
Better than the bitter butter,
Put it in the bitter batter,
Made the bitter batter better.
So 'twas better Betty Botta
Bought a bit of better butter.

A big baby buggy with rubber buggy bumpers.

A big black bug bleeds black blood.

How much wood would a woodchuck chuck
If a woodchuck could chuck wood?

He would chuck as much wood as a woodchuck could
If a woodchuck could chuck wood.

For more rhymes see:
A ROCKET IN MY POCKET. *Carl A. Withers. Holt, Rinehart & Winston. 1948.*

FINGER PLAYS

Knock at the Door I think this is about the oldest and simplest finger play there is, but modern babies respond to it as delightedly as old-time babies did.

Knock at the door,
(GENTLY KNOCK ON THE BABY'S FOREHEAD)
    Peep in,
(TOUCH THE EYELID)
    Lift up the latch,
(TOUCH THE NOSE)
    And walk in!
(TOUCH—OR POINT TO—THE MOUTH)
    Chin-chopper-chin-chopper-chin!
(CHUCK THE BABY UNDER THE CHIN)

This Little Piggy

This is a variation of "This little pig went to market," for Baby's fingers or toes.

This little piggy stubbed his toe.
This little piggy said, "Oh! Oh!"
This little piggy laughed; he was bad.
This little piggy cried; he was sad.
This little piggy was *very* good;
He ran for the doctor as fast as he could.

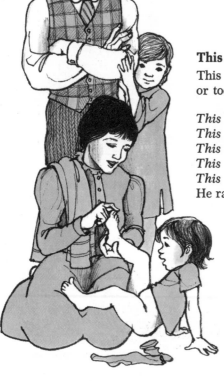

Houses

    Here is a nest for the robin,
(CUP TWO HANDS)
    Here is a hive for the bee,
(TWO FISTS TOGETHER)
    Here is a hole for the bunny,
(CIRCLE WITH FOREFINGERS AND THUMBS)
    And here is a house for me.
(FINGERTIPS TOGETHER TO MAKE A ROOF)

Tea Party
        Here's a cup, and here's a cup,
(MAKE FIST OF LEFT HAND, THEN RIGHT HAND)
        And here's a pot of tea.
(ADD SPOUT TO RIGHT HAND BY PROTRUDING THUMB)
        Pour a cup, and pour a cup,
(POUR INTO LEFT AND THEN RIGHT)
        And have a cup with me!
(EXTEND CUP TO NEIGHBOR AND PRETEND TO BE DRINKING)

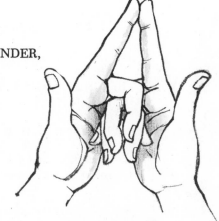

And don't forget:
        Here are my mother's knives and forks,
(PUT BACKS OF HANDS TOGETHER, LITTLE FINGERS NEXT TO CHEST, THUMBS OUT. INTERLACE FINGERS.)
        And here's my father's table.
(TURN INTERLACED FINGERS UNDER, WITH KNUCKLES FLAT ON TOP.)
        Here's my sister's rocking chair,
(TWO LITTLE FINGERS UP, WITH TIPS MEETING. ROCK BACK AND FORTH.)
        And here's the baby's cradle.
(FOREFINGERS UP, TIPS MEETING, ROCK SIDEWAYS.)

Here is another old favorite.
        This is the church,
(SECOND POSITION ABOVE, INTERLACED FINGERS UNDER, KNUCKLES FLAT ON TOP)
        And this is the steeple.
(FOREFINGERS UP, TIPS MEETING)
        Open the doors,
(SPREAD THUMBS WIDE APART.)
        And see all the people.
(TURN INTERLACED FINGERS TIPS UP.)

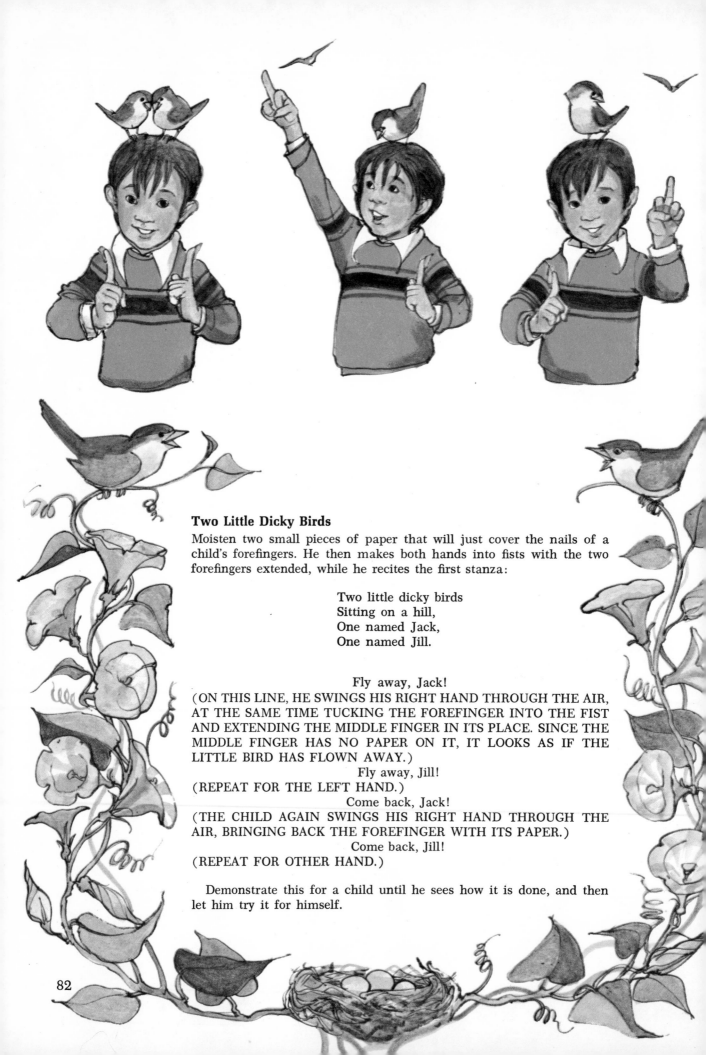

Two Little Dicky Birds

Moisten two small pieces of paper that will just cover the nails of a child's forefingers. He then makes both hands into fists with the two forefingers extended, while he recites the first stanza:

> Two little dicky birds
> Sitting on a hill,
> One named Jack,
> One named Jill.

> Fly away, Jack!

(ON THIS LINE, HE SWINGS HIS RIGHT HAND THROUGH THE AIR, AT THE SAME TIME TUCKING THE FOREFINGER INTO THE FIST AND EXTENDING THE MIDDLE FINGER IN ITS PLACE. SINCE THE MIDDLE FINGER HAS NO PAPER ON IT, IT LOOKS AS IF THE LITTLE BIRD HAS FLOWN AWAY.)

> Fly away, Jill!

(REPEAT FOR THE LEFT HAND.)

> Come back, Jack!

(THE CHILD AGAIN SWINGS HIS RIGHT HAND THROUGH THE AIR, BRINGING BACK THE FOREFINGER WITH ITS PAPER.)

> Come back, Jill!

(REPEAT FOR OTHER HAND.)

Demonstrate this for a child until he sees how it is done, and then let him try it for himself.

Two Little Owls

Two little owls on the telephone line,
Sitting straight as pokers, eyes all shine!
(THUMBS UP, FOREFINGERS MEETING)
Said one to the other, "What shall we do?"
(RIGHT THUMB BENT IN)
Said the other to the one, "Let's sing 'Who? Who?'"
(LEFT THUMB IN, THEN HANDS ON EACH SIDE OF MOUTH,
PALMS OUT)
Two little owls singing in the night
(FIRST POSITION)
On the telephone line—They held on tight!
(CLENCHED FISTS AS THOUGH CLINGING TO WIRE)
Two little owls sang the night away,
(FIRST POSITION)
Then they snuggled in their feathers and slept all day.
(ARMS CROSSED ON CHEST, FINGERS ON SHOULDERS. THEN
LET HEAD FALL FORWARD, EYES CLOSED.)

Alice White North
(Used by permission)

Eensie Teensie Spider

    An eensie teensie spider
    Went up the water spout.
(FOREFINGER OF LEFT HAND TO TIP OF RIGHT THUMB; FORE-
FINGER OF RIGHT HAND TO TIP OF LEFT THUMB. KEEP ALTER-
NATING TO IMITATE SPIDER'S CLIMB, IN TIME TO RHYTHM OF
SONG)
    Down came the rain and
    Washed the spider out.
(WAVE HANDS UP AND DOWN TO IMITATE FALLING RAIN.)
    Out came the sun and
    Dried up all the rain.
(ARMS MAKE BIG CIRCLE.)
    Then the eensie teensie spider
    Went up the spout again.
(SAME ACTION AS AT BEGINNING.)

    For the smallest, give help in finger action at beginning and end. Or
let them do what comes naturally.

Other Things To Do

READING AND STORYTELLING

Richer than I you can never be—
I had a mother who read to me.
　　　　Strickland Gillilan in
　　　　"The Reading Mother"

Reading is, of course, one of the most rewarding activities anybody can engage in. Even babies enjoy being read to, and the earlier they are introduced to books, the better. When they graduate from the first cloth books, they can be encouraged to treat all books kindly. They will respect them if they see that those around them do.

When Robert begins reading for himself, he may occasionally like to play "You read to me; I read to you," taking turns with an adult. This is especially good for a *reluctant* reader, for it makes an opportunity for that important one-to-one relationship and lets him see that grown-ups consider reading an interesting occupation. If necessary, you can declare "short turns" or "long turns" in the reading game, with the grown-up taking the long turns. Treat it as fun, not a chore.

Bev tells me about a variation of "You read to me; I read to you" that works with some children. You add an action game to it by suggesting that when Reluctant Reader does well with his page (doesn't miss too many words), his reward is to ask you to do a trick (stand on your head, make him a milkshake, turn a somersault). If he misses too many *you* ask *him* to do the trick. All this helps to make the reading time more exciting.

A trip to the library where Robert can pick out his own books is a good idea. If he selects books that are too difficult for him to read for himself, go ahead and read them *to* him. The important thing is to keep him interested, at the same time steering him toward *some* books that he can read for himself.*

* For stories that beginners can read, see THE READ-IT-YOURSELF STORYBOOK, *Leland B. Jacobs,* ed. *Western. 1971.*

Throughout this book there are activities that are fun to do and at the same time can also be painless helps to children who are having reading problems.

Bedtime seems the natural time for reading to the very young, but as children grow older and activities multiply, that ritual disappears. When Nell and Dale outgrew the bedtime story hour, we found another time. They washed the dinner dishes in the evening, and the time passed more pleasantly for everyone if I read to them. No more arguments about whether a spoon was clean! Just *My Friend Flicka, The Count of Monte Cristo, A Tale of Two Cities, The Three Musketeers!* There are so many books that families can enjoy together. And don't tell me the electric dishwasher eliminates this time, because there is still the clearing-the-table and putting-away-food time. I have yet to see the dishwasher that does those tasks. You

might find other duties (dusting, silver and furniture polishing, for instance) that could be accomplished with infinitely more joy to the tune of a good book.

A "natural" reader needs no encouragement, but you can still play an important part in a child's development by introducing him to certain books when you think he is ready for them. Frances Hodgson Burnett's *The Secret Garden* seems to interest today's children as much as it did when it was published in 1911, but don't be surprised if all your enthusiasms aren't shared by the youngsters. Your part is to expose children to the best books you know, and knowing your child usually helps you to know what ones he will enjoy.

Storytelling, like reading, can be started with babies. Children like stories or rhymes that have action parts that they can help the storyteller to demonstrate.

The Bear Hunt
(Both Jessie Morgan and Bev Vance demonstrate this very effectively.)

The old "Bear Hunt" story is an example of a special kind of story-telling, involving action and participation. You can tell this to one child, but it is more exciting with several.

Sit down in front of the children, who can be on the floor or on chairs —in any position where they can pat one knee and then the other.

Leader: Have you ever been on a bear hunt?
Children: No. (Or if somebody says "Yes," that's all right, too.)
Leader: Everything that I say you say after me; and everything that I do, you do. Everybody ready?
(Put one hand on each of your knees, and look around to see that the children have done the same.)
Leader: Let's go on a bear hunt.
Children: Let's go on a bear hunt. (Get children to repeat each statement.)
(Leader rhythmically pats one knee and then the other, to indicate slow walking, and children imitate, in unison.)
Leader (shading eyes with hand and peering into distance): Oh, look!
(Children repeat and imitate action.)
Leader: I see a *river*.
(Children repeat.)
Leader: Can't go *around* it.
(Children repeat.)
Leader: Can't go *under* it.
(Children repeat.)
Leader (making breast-stroke motions): Let's *swim* across.
(After four or five swimming strokes, resume knee-patting. Children repeat and imitate action.)
Leader (hand over eyes again): Oh. look!
(From here on, as in preceding part, Leader pauses after each line for children to repeat the words, and imitate each action.)

I see a *fence*.
Can't go *around* it.
Can't go *under* it.

Let's climb *over*. (Make climbing motions—up, then down. Resume patting.)

Oh, look! (Hand over eyes again)

I see a *wheat field* (corn, cane, or cotton field—or whatever grows tall where you live)

Can't go *around* it.

Can't go *under* it.

Let's go *through*. (Place palms of hands together and move back and forth briskly to make a swishing sound. Then resume patting.)

Oh, look! (Hand over eyes again)

I see a *cave*.

Can't go *over* it.

Can't go *under* it.

Let's go *inside* and explore. (Patting slows down and is done quietly.)

Oooh! It's dark in here. (Reach out hands as if feeling sides and roof of cave.)

It's *cold*.

It's *hard*.

It's *damp*. (Hands reach downward, feeling around.)

I feel something *soft*.

It's *warm*.

It's *furry*.

It's a BEAR!

Let's run.

(Do all the pantomime in reverse: very fast patting for running, then the swish-swish for the field, then fast patting again, climbing motions for the fence, fast patting again, swimming motions for the river, fast patting again, and then end up with arms crossed on chest and hands on shoulders, hugging yourself.)

Back home, safe!

Get a couple of children to practice this with you until you can do it easily and without hesitation. As I have given it, it is river, fence, field; and then field, fence, river. You can substitute different obstacles and motions if you like.

DICTATING STORIES

If you can start little children dictating stories when they are very young, they will enjoy reading them when they are older—and oh, so much wiser!

Here are some samples that may be interesting because of the development they reveal:

Laura's stories

(At 3½)

Wintertime, wintertime!
Need your coat,
Need a cold blanket,
Need a hat,
Need a heater in the car.
Wintertime, wintertime!
Cold, cold, cold!

(At 4½)

A little man was walking to a house, and he saw a mean man, so he walked to another house. And then the little man walked to another house. Was that the same house? No. And that's what the man did. So he walked and he walked and he walked and he walked and he walked. Stop.

(At 5½)

Once upon a time there was a little girl, and she lived in the woods. And her mother and father lived with her. And she went out in the forest and she came to a tiger. And the tiger said, "What are you doing here?" And so the little girl ran back home and hugged her mother and father.

The Pumpkin and the Little Black Kitten

Once upon a time on a farm there was a pumpkin vine. On this vine there was a pumpkin that nobody could see from the other side.

One time the pumpkin saw a little black kitten coming out of the field. Then the pumpkin asked the little black kitten if she would take him off the vine because nobody would ever pick him for Hallowe'en.

After the little kitten picked him, they started down the road. Then they met a man and asked him if he would cut some eyes in the pumpkin. He just happened to have a knife so he cut some eyes.

Then they started down the road again and met a little old lady. They asked her if she would cut a nose for the pumpkin, so she did. After that, they said, "Thank you," and started down the road again.

After they had gone a little ways, they met a boy going fishing, and asked him if he would cut a mouth for the pumpkin. So he did.

It was getting close to Hallowe'en when they saw a little house. Before that, the pumpkin had said to the little kitten that he wanted a boy who whistled while he worked, and the kitten had said that she wanted a little girl with long brown hair and blue eyes.

In the house that they saw there was a little girl with blue eyes and long brown hair, and there was a boy that whistled while he worked.

The little girl saw the pumpkin and called her brother Jack to come and see what she had found. The little boy said that was what he wanted for Hallowe'en.

That night was Hallowe'en, and they put the pumpkin in the window. Then the little girl went up to the pumpkin to put a candle in it, when she saw the little black kitten inside the pumpkin.

She said, "This is what I want for Hallowe'en."

Jack and his sister Susie were both happy that Hallowe'en. So were the kitten and the pumpkin, and they all lived happily ever after.

Lynn's stories
(At 5)

Twinkle, twinkle, little star,
How do I sparkle so much?
I sparkle by the sun.
I sparkle by the moon.

(At 6)

There was this little brown house on a little gray street. But the street wasn't very busy. And they had five kids. There was this big field with a big sand pile, and the kids liked to play in the sand pile. They built big castles and big houses. And then they made roads all through the sand pile. And then late in the morning a big brown bear came, and the bear was sure nice. And so they played with it every morning and all day. And then at night they put it in the cage and put it to sleep. And then the next morning they woke it up and put on its clothes. And then they runned around in the yard and turned somersaults, and then they came in and ate lunch. And that's the end.

(At 7)

One time a little rabbit was cooking some stew outside of his little hole. And then he saw a great big lion coming. And then he ran down his hole. And then he ran down another hole. And then he ran down another hole. And then the lion said, "Uh, *huh!*" and he started digging, and just as he got to the bottom of the hole—that lion—the little rabbit was eating out the back of the hole. Then the little rabbit jumped up into a tree*—and then another tree. And then the lion climbed up in the tree, and all the little animals knew about it; and so they ate down the bottom of the tree, and then the tree fell on the lion, and the little rabbit got away all right because the lion was dead.

* When Grandmother said, "I didn't think rabbits could climb trees, Lynn answered, "Well, this one can, because it's a magic rabbit."

(At 8)   Tubby and the Weasel

Once there was a little bear named Tubby. He had two sisters and one brother. Tubby was the smallest bear of them all. He didn't mind his mother.

One day the mother bear said that they could go and pick flowers or fish in the lake. All the little bears did what their mother said except Tubby. Tubby went farther out into the woods, and there in the woods lived a mean old weasel.

This mean old weasel wanted to scare a little rabbit and eat it. But instead, he scared Tubby, and Tubby fell into the trap. It was getting darker and darker, and Tubby wanted to go home.

It happened that his mother was going into the forest to pick blueberries. Then all of a sudden she heard a noise. It was Tubby trying to warn his mother from falling into the trap. She looked down and saw Tubby. Then she took the rope off the bucket she was carrying and put it down into the hole and told Tubby to hold onto it. Then she pulled Tubby out. Then all of a sudden the weasel started coming back. The mother heard him, and they hid in the bushes.

While they were hiding, the mother tied the rope back on the bucket. She put the bucket down in the hole and covered it up with weeds. She told Tubby to go around on the other side, and she lifted her hand to push the weasel into the bucket. Then they came out of their hiding place and pulled the weasel up out of the hole, and the weasel never bothered them again. Then they went on their way and picked blueberries, and when they got home the children were fixing their supper, and Tubby always minded his mother after that.

At the time of these last stories, Lynn and Laura could write for themselves, but they liked to dictate because, as Lynn said, "I can think more about the story instead of about the writing." Gradually, as the physical act of putting words on paper became easier for them, they gave up dictating, but that early practice (or so I like to think) has made it easier for them to tell a story orally.

MUSIC FUN

Listening Music, like storytelling, can be introduced to children very early in life. First, mother sings to baby. Then come records of Mother Goose and nursery songs — and "serious" music, too. It is not too much to say that babies and children may like any kind of music *you* like to listen to.

Pantomime Children often like to sing along with a record. You can show them how to pantomine — to "sing without making any sound," exaggerating movements of the lips and tongue, and adding any melodramatic gestures your little hams can think up.

Homemade rhythm bands If you can stand the racket, pot lids and spoons make good percussion instruments. Less noisy are wooden bowls and spoons. Let your children improvise instruments (rulers, pencils, etc.) to keep time with music they are listening to. And, of course, there is still the old-fashioned "musical comb" — made by putting a piece of tissue paper over a comb and humming a tune against it.

Rhythm game Clap (or tap) the rhythm of a tune familar to your listener, and have him guess what the song is and sing it. Then see if he can tap out a tune for you to guess.

Conducting an orchestra and dancing to music Encourage a child to "conduct" an orchestra that is playing on radio, record player, or television. Let him stand in front of the instrument with a pencil for a baton. If it is one of the rare times a symphony orchestra is shown on television, the child can imitate the actual conductor. If he is only hearing, and not seeing, he can make up appropriate motions. One child may want to conduct, while another child may prefer to make up a dance to the same music.

Musical glasses Debbie Locke reminds me that you can show children how to make music from drinking glasses containing water. The more water there is in the glass, the lower the tone. Help the children to "tune" the glasses. Fill one glass almost to the brim and let it represent *do* (or 1 in the diatonic scale). Then make each successive glass a little less full, striking the edge of the glass with a fork to hear the tone and adding or subtracting water until the sounds accurately represent the notes of the scale.

With six glasses representing *do, re, mi, fa, sol,* and *la,* (or 1, 2, 3, 4, 5, and 6) you can play "Twinkle, twinkle, little star." It goes:

1 — 1 — 5 — 5 — 6 — 6 — 5
4 — 4 — 3 — 3 — 2 — 2 — 1

By adding a glass or two at the top and bottom of the scale, you can play almost any simple tune.

If you have a piano, let your little ones try to pick out tunes when they show interest. But don't let them bang. Tell them a piano is for making music, not noise!

Instruments can often be rented during the period when children are exploring aptitudes and interests.

SOME HOBBIES TO EXPLORE

There are books on the subject of just about every hobby you can think of, and when you know a child's special interest, you can encourage it. You can also introduce him to new interests. Besides the hobbies suggested by the activities in this book, here are some of the many hobbies you may want to explore with your children.

"Making" hobbies
Clay modeling
Sculpture (including soap sculpture and wire sculpture)
Weaving, knitting, embroidery, macramé
Whittling and wood carving
Making designs or pictures with thumb tacks or nails on a piece of wood

Science hobbies
Growing things (gardening indoors and out)
A sweet potato, a pineapple top, an avocado pit, and citrus fruit seeds make interesting indoor plants.
Observing (and keeping records)
Animals and their habits (pets, wild animals, zoo animals)
Birds, fish in aquarium, flowers, insects, leaves, rocks, seeds, shells, trees, weeds
Weather

Collecting hobbies Postcards, stamps, coins, dolls, some of the items mentioned on page 94 under *Observing*, books or articles about a favorite hobby

Scrapbooks (sometimes simple file folders or manila envelopes to hold material of temporary interest; sometimes elaborate looseleaf notebooks which can grow into several volumes)

Suggested subjects: Birds (when and where seen)
Drawings or sketches
Ecology
Favorite poems
Items about space travel
Leaves (identified)
Planes, trains, trucks, or cars
Recipes
Stories of pets

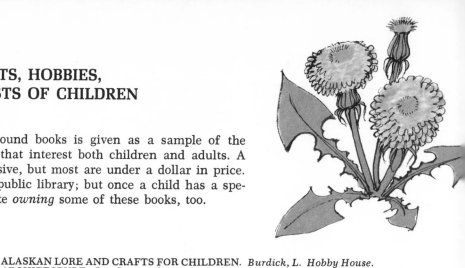

BOOKS ABOUT CRAFTS, HOBBIES, AND OTHER INTERESTS OF CHILDREN

The following list of paperbound books is given as a sample of the many books about activities that interest both children and adults. A few of these are more expensive, but most are under a dollar in price. The place to begin is in the public library; but once a child has a special interest, he will appreciate *owning* some of these books, too.

ALASKAN LORE AND CRAFTS FOR CHILDREN. *Burdick, L. Hobby House.*
ARCHITECTURE. *Boy Scouts of America. BSA.*
ARROW BOOK OF PUZZLES. *Rockowitz, M. Scholastic Book Services.*
ARROW BOOK OF SCIENCE RIDDLES. *Wyler, R. Scholastic Book Services.*
ASTRONOMY. *Boy Scouts of America. BSA.*
AVIATION. *Boy Scouts of America. BSA.*
BICYCLING. *Fichter, G. S. and Kingbay, K. Golden Press. Western.*
BIG BOOK OF PENCIL GAMES. *Peterson, H. M. Doubleday.*
BIOLOGY EXPERIMENTS FOR CHILDREN. *Hanauer, E. Dover.*
BIRDS. *Zim, H. S. and Gabrielson, I. N. Golden Press. Western.*
BOOK OF HORSES. *Balch, G. Scholastic Book Services.*
BOOK OF REAL SCIENCE. *Freeman, M. Scholastic Book Services.*
BOOKBINDING. *Boy Scouts of America. BSA.*
BOTANY. *Boy Scouts of America. BSA.*
BOTANY. *Alexander, T., Burnett, R. W., and Zim, H. S. Golden Press. Western.*
BUTTERFLIES AND MOTHS. *Zim, H. S. and Mitchell, R. Golden Press. Western.*
CATS. *Fichter, G. S. Golden Press. Western.*
CHEMISTRY. *Boy Scouts of America. BSA.*
CHEMISTRY EXPERIMENTS FOR CHILDREN. *Mullin, V. L. Dover.*
CHILD'S PRIMER OF NATURAL HISTORY. *Herford, O. Dover.*
COIN COLLECTING. *Boy Scouts of America. BSA.*
COUNTING OUT RHYMES. *Withers, C. Dover.*
CREATIVE CRAFTS FOR CHILDREN. *Beson, K. R. Prentice Hall.*
CROSSWORDS FOR KIDS. *White, L. Fawcett. World.*
DO IT YOURSELF: TRICKS, STUNTS & SKITS. *Carlson, B. W. Abingdon.*
ECOLOGY. *Alexander, T. and Fichter, G. S. Golden Press. Western.*
EIGHTEEN HUNDRED RIDDLES, ENIGMAS & CONUNDRUMS. *Hindman, D. A. Dover.*
ELECTRICITY. *Boy Scouts of America. BSA.*
FIND OUT FOR YOURSELF. *Price, E. Zondervan.*
FINGERPRINTING. *Boy Scouts of America. BSA.*
FISHES. *Zim, H. S. and Shoemaker, H. H. Golden Press. Western.*
FISHING. *McNally, T. Follett.*
FLOWERS. *Zim, H. S. and Martin, A. C. Golden Press. Western.*
FOSSILS. *Rhodes, F. H. T., Shaffer, P. R., and Zim, H. S. Golden Press. Western.*
GAMES FOR BOYS AND GIRLS. *Harbin, E. O. Abingdon.*
GARDENING. *Boy Scouts of America. BSA.*
GEOLOGY. *Boy Scouts of America. BSA.*
GOLF FOR BOYS AND GIRLS. *Cromie, R. A. Follett.*
GYMNASTICS FOR BOYS. *Bedard, I. Follett*
HAND SHADOWS. *Bursill, H. Dover.*
HOW TO CARE FOR YOUR DOG. *Bethell, J. Scholastic Book Services.*
INDIAN ARTS. *Whiteford, A. H. Golden Press. Western.*
INDIAN SIGN LANGUAGE. *Tomkins, W. Dover.*
INSECTS. *Zim, H. S. and Cottam, C. A. Golden Press. Western.*
IT'S FUN TO MAKE THINGS FROM SCRAP MATERIALS. *Hershoff, E. G. Dover.*
KITES. *Brummitt, W. Golden Press. Western.*
LEATHERWORK. *Boy Scouts of America. BSA.*
LET'S DRAW ANIMALS. *Davidow, A. Grossett & Dunlap.*
LIFESAVING. *Boy Scouts of America. BSA.*
MAKE IT AND USE IT. *Carlson, B. W. Abingdon.*
MAKE IT YOURSELF. *Carlson, B. W. Abingdon.*
MAMMALS. *Zim, H. S. and Hoffmeister, D. F. Golden Press. Western.*
METALWORK. *Boy Scouts of America. BSA.*
MODEL DESIGN AND BUILDING. *Boy Scouts of America. BSA.*
MORE HANDCRAFTS AND FUN. *Doan, E. Zondervan.*
OCEANOGRAPHY. *Boy Scouts of America. BSA.*
PENCIL PASTIMES. *Lewis, R. Doubleday.*
PHOTOGRAPHY. *Boy Scouts of America. BSA.*
PHYSICS EXPERIMENTS FOR CHILDREN. *Mandell, M. Dover.*
PIGEON RAISING. *Boy Scouts of America. BSA.*
PLANETS. *Lauber, P. Random House.*
PLAY WITH DOTS. *Thompson, M. Doubleday.*
PLUMBING. *Boy Scouts of America. BSA.*
POETRY IS. *Hughes, T. Doubleday.*
POND LIFE. *Reid, G. K. Golden Press. Western.*
POTTERY. *Boy Scouts of America. BSA.*
PRINTING. *Boy Scouts of America. BSA.*
PUFFIN BOOK OF LETTERING. *Gourdie, T. Penguin.*
RABBIT RAISING. *Boy Scouts of America. BSA.*

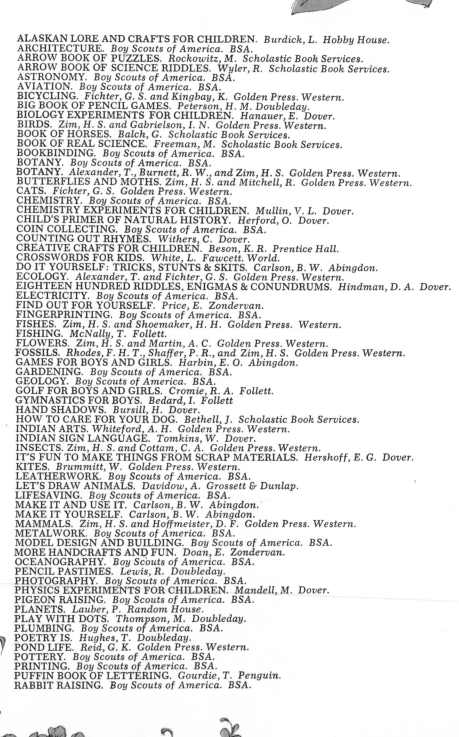

RADIO. *Boy Scouts of America. BSA.*
RAINY DAY BOOK. *Schwartz, A. Pocket Books.*
READING. *Boy Scouts of America. BSA.*
REAL MAGNET BOOK. *Freeman, M. Scholastic Book Services.*
REPTILE STUDY. *Boy Scouts of America. BSA.*
REPTILES AND AMPHIBIANS. *Zim, H. S. and Smith, H. M. Golden Press. Western.*
ROCKET BOOK. *Newell, P. Dover.*
ROCKS. *Zim, H. S. and Shaffer, P. R. Golden Press. Western.*
SAFETY. *Boy Scouts of America. BSA.*
SCIENCE IN YOUR OWN BACK YARD. *Cooper, E. K. Voyager Books. Harcourt Brace
    Jovanovich.*
SCRAP CRAFT: 105 PROJECTS. *Dank, M. C. Dover.*
SEASHELLS OF THE WORLD. *Abbott, R. T. Golden Press. Western.*
SESAME STREET BOOK OF PUZZLERS. *Ed. by Children's TV Workshop. Signet Books.
    New American Library, Inc.*
SIGNALING. *Boy Scouts of America. BSA.*
SKIING. *Boy Scouts of America. BSA.*
SMALL-BOAT SAILING. *Boy Scouts of America. BSA.*
SPIDERS AND THEIR KIN. *Levi, H. and L. Golden Press. Western.*
STAMP COLLECTING. *Boy Scouts of America. BSA.*
STARS. *Zim, H. S. and Baker, R. H. Golden Press. Western.*
SURVEYING. *Boy Scouts of America. BSA.*
SWIMMING. *Boy Scouts of America. BSA.*
TANGRAMS: 330 PUZZLES. *Read, R. C. Dover.*
TEXTILES. *Boy Scouts of America. BSA.*
TREES. *Zim, H. S. and Martin, A. C. Golden Press. Western.*
WEATHER. *Burnett, R. W., Lehr, P. E., and Zim, H. S. Golden Press. Western.*
WEEDS. *Martin, A. C. Golden Press. Western.*
WHITTLING AND WOODCARVING. *Tangerman, E. J. Dover.*
WONDERS OF SEEDS. *Stefferud, A. Voyager Books. Harcourt Brace Jovanovich.*
WOOD CARVING. *Boy Scouts of America. BSA.*
WOODWORK. *Boy Scouts of America. BSA.*
WORLD OF BOOKS. *Chaffin, L. D. and Simon, R. C., Jr. Children's Press.*
ZOO ANIMALS. *Zim, H. S. and Hoffmeister, D. F. Golden Press. Western.*
ZOOLOGY. *Boy Scouts of America. BSA.*

TRAVEL

Travel Aids

Flying across the Atlantic from Glasgow to New York, I once delightedly observed a young Scottish couple with two little girls. By bringing along a set of finger puppets and two small books (Father had one in his pocket; Mother had one in her purse), the parents showed they realized that a transatlantic plane ride doesn't provide much entertainment for pre-school children. They had prepared for the trip by remembering a favorite toy and two favorite books.

No matter whether you travel by family car, bus, train, plane, or ship, a little foresight will pay big dividends in keeping everyone in good spirits.

Here are some items that are good to have along when traveling with a child:

Small pair of blunt-ended kindergarten scissors
Pencil
Crayons or colored pencils
A few sheets of plain or colored paper
Deck of cards
Two or three business envelopes (to hold tangrams or paper dolls or snowflakes that children make)
Extra cloth handkerchiefs for handkerchief magic
Twenty or thirty dried beans for playing *Hull Gull* (Keep them in an envelope or paper bag)
Newspaper (for newspaper magic and for catching "crumbs")
This book *The Everything Book*

IMAGINATION STRETCHERS

Make up games to suit the occasion. Such games are something like extended conversation pieces. Here are a few suggestions to get you started.

The "seeing things in the clouds" game As you move along, the clouds are constantly changing and suggesting new shapes. Players describe and point out to each other the things they see.

A naming game Name five new things you saw in the airport, in the last town, since we left home, in the station, on this train, etc.

"Thinking" games Think up uses for a common object like a toothpaste cap. (In fantasy: "a water glass for Thumbelina," "a flower pot" or "a waste basket" or "a lampshade" or "a bucket" for different dollhouses; or in reality: "to serve as an emergency thimble" or "to plug up a hole in a leaky boat.")

Think of an appropriate gift for the President, a football hero, a well-known baseball player, a television star, a character from a book, someone you know, or anyone else that players suggest.

VARIATIONS Think of a good hobby, game, sport, or book for any of the above (or others).

Make up a menu for any of the above (favorite foods for someone you like, unfavorite foods for unfavorite people).

A listening game Keep still and listen for 60 seconds. Then name everything you could hear during the listening time.

The "what do you suppose?" game One player asks, "What do you suppose makes an airplane stay up in the air?" or "What do you suppose makes it fly?" The other players explain the principles of aerodynamics as best they can. The adult corrects any misconceptions—if he can! If not, he makes a mental note to look up the subject, or makes plans with the children to consult an authority. The encouragement of curiosity and interest is more important than knowing the answer at that particular moment. Other questions might be: "Why do you suppose people have different-colored skin?" "Why do you suppose people fight wars?" "Where do you suppose ants go in winter?" "Where do you suppose I could buy an ice cream cone right now?" "Where do you suppose Robin Hood would like to live if he came back to life?" etc.

A color game Leader says, "Red," and players name everything they can think of that is red—fire engine, tomato, flag stripes, etc. When the answers slow down, switch to other colors.

VARIATION FOR OLDER CHILDREN What does a color suggest? Red might be anger, heat, fire, excitement, etc.

Simile sentences Start sentences (for players to finish) that require them to think in terms of simile. For example,

Walking in dry leaves sounds like . . .
Rain sounds like . . .
The wind sounds like . . .
The hot sun feels like . . .
Petting a kitten feels like . . .
A cold shower feels like . . .
Snow looks like . . .
Ice cream tastes like . . .
Bread baking smells like . . .

Let each player finish the sentence as he likes; stop the game before players get bored. Some children may want a turn at starting sentences for others to finish.

REMEMBERING GAMES

Especially for a family traveling by car, there are many kinds of remembering games (remembering songs, poems, proverbs, quotations), and most of them can be played in any kind of conveyance. One quotation game we used to enjoy goes like this: The first player says, for instance, "Into each life some rain must fall." Then whoever can think of a quotation beginning with *f* (the first letter of the last word) says, "Fourscore and seven years ago . . . ," and so on.

Singing in a car is fun for all ages. Because children get tired of sitting still, choose plenty of action songs like *Looby Loo* (p. 61), *Did You Ever See a Lassie?* (p. 62), *She'll Be Comin' Round the Mountain* (p. 62), *John Brown's Baby* (p. 67), and *The Eeensie Teensie Spider* (p. 84). Because dialogue between front seat and back seat, or between males and females is fun, choose songs like *A Hole in the Bucket* (p. 66) and *Lazy Mary* (p. 67).

Finger plays give the same opportunity for motion when children are restless. Think of ways to use rhymes and riddles.

OTHER TRAVEL GAMES

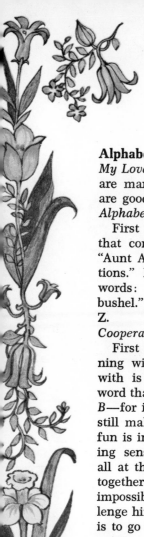

Alphabet games In addition to *I Love My Love with an A* (See Index), there are many other alphabet games that are good for travel.

Alphabet sentences

First player makes up a sentence that contains at least five *A* words: "Aunt Agnes always asks awful questions." Next player goes on with *B* words: "Betsy buys berries by the bushel." And so on, omitting *Q, X,* and *Z.*

Cooperative alphabet story

First player says one word, beginning with *A.* A good word to begin with is A. The next player adds a word that makes sense, beginning with *B*—for instance, *big.* The next player, still making sense, may add *cat.* The fun is in following the alphabet, making sense, and trying for continuity all at the same time. Everyone works together. If someone wants to add an impossible word, the others may challenge him to explain how the sentence is to go on. Eventually, of course, one sentence has to end, and another begins.

Variation

Have each player continue until he finishes a sentence. If you want to keep score, give one point for each word. Then the player will try to go on as far as he can before finishing the sentence. For instance, Alan might say, "A big city dog, exceedingly fat, galloped hotly into Janet's kitchen." (11 points for Alan) Then Lois might go on, " 'Look, Mother, no onions, potatoes, quail, radishes!' said the ugly varmint with x-tremely youthful zeal." (15 points for Lois) Be lenient about X.

Here are a few more examples:

"A brown chocolate donkey, eating fat greasy ham in jail, kicked Little Mister Nonno over Patsy's queer roof. Soon the unlucky veteran wanted X-rays, yawning zanily."

"After Brother Charles dared excited Florence Green, he impishly jumped, kicking like mad. Next old Polly Queen ran, sliding through unarmed villages with xylophones, yelling 'Zero!' "

This is a hard game, but some older children enjoy the challenge. At home, it's permissible to use a dictionary, but you'll have to get along without it when traveling. (If you make it a writing game, you'll have more time to think.)

Alphabet categories

One player names a category (fruit, boys' names, adjectives, trees, etc.). Immediately, someone calls out an *A* word in the category—for instance, *apricot* for fruit. Another player goes on with *B,* then *C.* etc. (Or players can take turns in order.) As soon as players get through the alphabet, another category is named, and the alphabet starts over.

Cumulative alphabet story

First player says, "I'm going on a trip and I'm going to take an *a*pple." Second player says, "I'm going on a trip and I'm going to take an *a*pple and a *b*ook." Third player says, "I'm going on a trip and I'm going to take an *a*pple and a *b*ook and a *c*alendar." And so on through the alphabet, each player repeating everything that has been said before. If a player gives up on remembering a word, he gets one minus point. The player with fewest minus points wins. Or—play without any penalties and let players prompt each other.

See if you can make up other alphabet games. For example:

Look for letters of the alphabet in sequence. In towns this is easy because of signs. In the country, you can use objects that start with the needed letter—animal for *A,* boy for *B,* cow for *C,* etc. Make any rules you need (like skipping Q, X, and Z if you like) before you begin. Everyone can work together. Even the youngest children can play if the older ones help by telling them what to look for.

Twenty Questions *Twenty Questions* may be played in the regular way of having all players except "It" agree on a person, place, or thing. (This has to be done by whispered consultation.) Then "It" asks questions that can be answered by "Yes" or "No," such as "Are you thinking of a man?" "Is he living?" "Is he an athlete?" "Is he a baseball player?" Players take turns answering. If "It" guesses in twenty questions or fewer, he wins.

Perhaps a better way to play is for the players to take turns choosing the person, place, or thing. For instance, Linda may decide on the Astrodome. All others (in turn) ask questions. Linda answers "Yes" or "No," and keeps track of the number of questions asked. If the others guess in twenty (or fewer) questions, everyone but Linda gets a point. If they *don't* guess, then it is Linda who scores.

Hand Is Foot, Foot Is Hand Let's say that Paul is first. He touches his hand and says, "This is my foot." Then he quickly points to Jill and begins counting to ten. Before he gets to ten, Jill must do the exact *opposite*—that is, she must touch her foot and say, "This is my hand." If she does it in time, she becomes "It," perhaps touching her wrist and saying, "This is my elbow." Then she points to Don, who must touch his elbow and say, "This is my wrist." If Don doesn't make the right response within the count of ten, Jill gets another turn. It is easy to devise a way of scoring, but this game is more fun if you don't bother about scoring. Just keep the game moving fast. It gives travelers a chance to do a lot of wiggling and laughing.

Continued story The first player begins a story: "A man was walking down a road in the dark. He saw a strange light coming from a house. As he came nearer, he heard . . ." As the storyteller breaks off, he points to someone else, and that person must pick up the thread of the story and go on: ". . . a scream. The man ran toward the house, but just before he got there the front door burst open, and out ran . . ." And so it goes on. You may not get a well-connected tale, but you *will* get some excitement.

Stone, Paper, Scissors (for two players) Players take turns counting, "One, two, three—show!" At the word, "show," each player extends a hand in one of the following positions: a clenched fist (stone), hand flat (paper), or two fingers in scissors position. Stone breaks scissors, scissors cut paper; and paper wraps stone. For instance, suppose Debbie shows her hand flat (paper) and David shows a clenched fist (stone). Debbie wins because paper wraps stone. If Debbie shows the scissors position, and David the clenched fist, then it is David who wins, because stone breaks scissors. If both show the same position, it's a tie, and they count again.

Score one point for each win. Before starting, decide what the winning score will be (whoever gets ten wins first—or twenty). This can be played very quickly.

10.
The End

MAGIC NUMBERS

The "Ten Eighty-nine" trick

	Examples	a	b	c
Write a number of three figures, with a difference of more than one between the first and third.		917	148	552
Write the same number backwards.		719	841	255
Subtract the smaller from the larger.		198	693	297
Write this last number backwards.		891	396	792
Add the last two numbers in each column and you will always get "ten eighty-nine!"		1089	1089	1089

The "How Old Are You?" trick
(All but the youngest can do this in their heads.)

	Examples	a	b	c
Tell each child to think of his age.		11	9	16
Multiply it by 3.		33	27	48
Add 1.		34	28	49
Multiply the answer by 3.		102	84	147
Add his age again.		113	93	163

Cross off the last figure on the right, and he will have his age. (It works, of course, for any age.)

QUICK TRICK

Suggest that all passengers rub their heads and pat their stomachs. Just when they are able to do it, suggest that they reverse the action and pat their heads while rubbing their stomachs.

ESPECIALLY FOR TRAVEL IN A CAR (OR BUS)

Racing raindrops This is a game I made up for Nell and Dale to play when they were very young. We were making a long drive in pouring rain, and they were tired of other games and wanted a new one. So I suggested that they each choose a raindrop at the top of the window on one side of the car, and watch to see whose "horse" would win the race by getting to the bottom of the window first. Sometimes a drop would start out very fast, only to stop halfway and be overtaken by a slow starter.

Such games may be good for only a few minutes, but they can change the mood of a rainy day. Encourage children to make up their own games.

License-plate games Look for numbers in sequence on license plates. Start with 1, and get a 2 on the same plate if it is there, but don't go on to 3 until you get a 2. When you get a 9, the game ends. This is best played co-operatively, with everyone but the driver looking for numbers.

See how many different states you can collect. Let one member of the family write down the names, with marks to indicate the frequency if they like.

See how many colors you can collect. This can be colors of cars and/or colors of license plates.

Other car games Look for horses or cows or white houses or anything you decide on ahead of time. Half the players take one side of the car, half another. When you come to a cemetery on your side, you have to bury your horses (or whatever) and start over. Whichever side gets ten horses first, wins.

104

FOR PARENTS TO KEEP IN MIND

Children love to learn new things. Take advantage of this in traveling. Point out to the youngest that STOP signs are always eight-sided, YIELD signs are triangular, etc. When you are trying to find a particular place, enlist the help of passengers.

Provide very young children with newspaper (for tearing snowflakes or paper dolls) if older children are playing games that are difficult. Be ready to suggest new games when children become restless. Encourage a child who likes to draw, to sketch along the way; one who likes to write, to keep a journal of the trip; one who likes numbers, to keep track of mileage or expenses.

When our two children were small, we traveled about fifty miles to my sister's home quite often. I remember how many times Nell would ask, "Are we closer to home, or closer to Aunt Mary's?" This made me think of challenging travelers with guessing games like, "How many miles do you suppose we have traveled today?" ("since we left home?" "since noon yesterday?" etc.) "How many miles will it take to get us where we are going today?"

Mary Frances Slack says the best pastime for car travel with children is reading aloud from a good book. David, Nancy, and Jeff range in age from ten to fifteen, and there are many books in this age range that can be enjoyed by everyone in the family—including mother and father.

For the youngest A small paper bag tied with a short string to the door handle of the car will flutter and dance in the breeze, and give a small traveler something to watch when he gets bored.

For stops Take along a jump rope, a top, or a ball to provide exercise for stops. Or let children run a race in a field.

Think up things to look for. Ask who can see the tallest tree, the largest or smallest rock, etc.

Hint Always keep a few newspapers in the trunk of the car. They have many uses—from making a tablecloth for a roadside table to providing the raw material for newspaper magic. (See index.)

SOUVENIRS

Remind your travelers of souvenirs of the mind and heart rather than junk. For instance:

A snapshot of a lovely scene (Or "take a picture with your eyes" — just stand still and look hard in order to carry away a peaceful or exciting landscape in your memory.)

A map of an area

A rock or a piece of mineral for your collection or for a friend's collection

A gift for an upcoming birthday of a relative or friend.

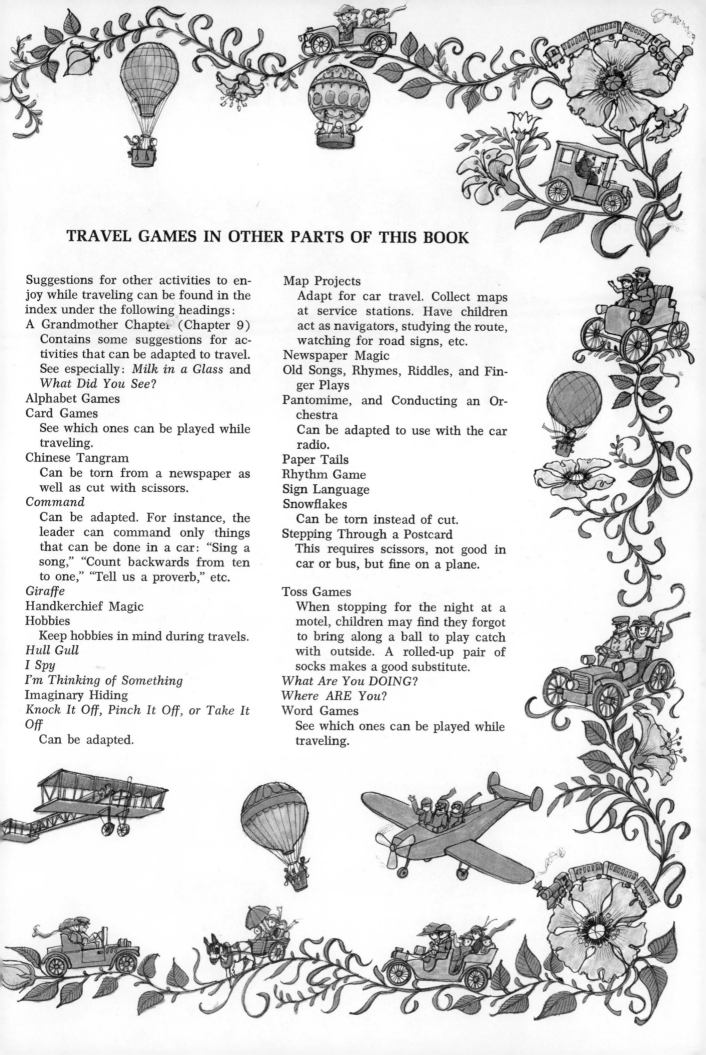

TRAVEL GAMES IN OTHER PARTS OF THIS BOOK

Suggestions for other activities to enjoy while traveling can be found in the index under the following headings:

A Grandmother Chapter (Chapter 9)
Contains some suggestions for activities that can be adapted to travel. See especially: *Milk in a Glass* and *What Did You See?*

Alphabet Games

Card Games
See which ones can be played while traveling.

Chinese Tangram
Can be torn from a newspaper as well as cut with scissors.

Command
Can be adapted. For instance, the leader can command only things that can be done in a car: "Sing a song," "Count backwards from ten to one," "Tell us a proverb," etc.

Giraffe

Handkerchief Magic

Hobbies
Keep hobbies in mind during travels.

Hull Gull

I Spy

I'm Thinking of Something

Imaginary Hiding

Knock It Off, Pinch It Off, or Take It Off
Can be adapted.

Map Projects
Adapt for car travel. Collect maps at service stations. Have children act as navigators, studying the route, watching for road signs, etc.

Newspaper Magic

Old Songs, Rhymes, Riddles, and Finger Plays

Pantomime, and Conducting an Orchestra
Can be adapted to use with the car radio.

Paper Tails

Rhythm Game

Sign Language

Snowflakes
Can be torn instead of cut.

Stepping Through a Postcard
This requires scissors, not good in car or bus, but fine on a plane.

Toss Games
When stopping for the night at a motel, children may find they forgot to bring along a ball to play catch with outside. A rolled-up pair of socks makes a good substitute.

What Are You DOING?

Where ARE You?

Word Games
See which ones can be played while traveling.

CONVALESCENCE

When a child is acutely ill, nursing is the important thing. But convalescence has special problems — problems that can be turned into opportunities for helping a child find interesting things to do while he is laid up.

First, of course, you will consult with the doctor and find out just how much activity is good for the patient. Reading to a child is probably the best way to keep him quiet and happy. And when he is able, he can read to himself, or look at picture books.

Most games require your presence unless there is someone else for the child to play with. But some of the suggestions in this chapter are for one child alone. You can supply materials and then alternate between activities that require you to stay in the sickroom and those that permit you to come and go.

Alphabet games Look in the index for alphabet games. For a youngster new to reading and new to the alphabet, just remembering *any* words in alphabetical order—*and, but, cat, dog*—is a challenging proposition. Help your child tailor the game to his expanding capabilities and interests by making up different categories to use. At one time, these can be concrete things: *trees* (ash, birch, coconut); *flowers* (dahlia, edelweiss, foxglove); *food* (grapes, hamburger, ice cream); *birds* (jay, kingfisher, lark). At another time, it can be adjectives or adverbs. The game can be oral or written. Children usually enjoy it more when they think up their own categories, and in that way the old game can be endlessly new.

TOSS GAMES

Even a bed patient can play toss games if he is permitted the exercise.

Toss playing cards or rubber jar rings into a box.

Toss a button or a penny into an egg carton or muffin tin. If the player wants to, he can declare the holes on the ends of the carton or tin worth ten points, and those in the middle worth five points. Keeping score — so many points out of so many tries — makes the game more interesting and gives the player a record to break.

Toss a rolled pair of socks into a waste basket.

The first two of the above toss games are played with the receptacle about two feet from the player, presumably on his bed.

With rolled socks or a ball of yarn as a substitute ball, you can place the waste basket on the floor about three feet from the bed. Tie a five-foot length of string firmly around the sock ball and pin the free end of the string to the pillow. Then the tosser can retrieve the ball by pulling in the string.

Or toss a rolled pair of socks (tied on a longer string) at a mirror target.

A mirror target can be made by patting talcum powder thickly in one spot on the mirror to make a bull's-eye. Make sure the string is more than long enough to reach the target. You won't want to do this if there are medicine bottles or other obstacles in the "line of fire," but a child restricted to bed appreciates any possible enlargement of his arena, so be as ingenious as you can in making up safe targets. When I was little I was often a bed patient, and my times in the children's ward taught me that a patient can remain technically "in bed," when he is really nine-tenths out!

Hand shadows A flashlight or a small high-intensity lamp is good for making hand shadows, because it can be easily moved about; but any portable light will do. If there is no blank wall space near the bed, pull up a chair and place a folded sheet over its back. Let the child figure out for himself how to adjust the light to make the best shadows.

VARIATION Ask your patient to hold still long enough for you to draw his silhouette. Pin a large piece of wrapping paper to the sheet, adjust the light to make a sharp outline of the child's profile, and draw it quickly. He may ask to "do" you next.

Chinese tangram To make a Chinese tangram, you need only a square of paper, a pencil, a ruler, and a pair of scissors.

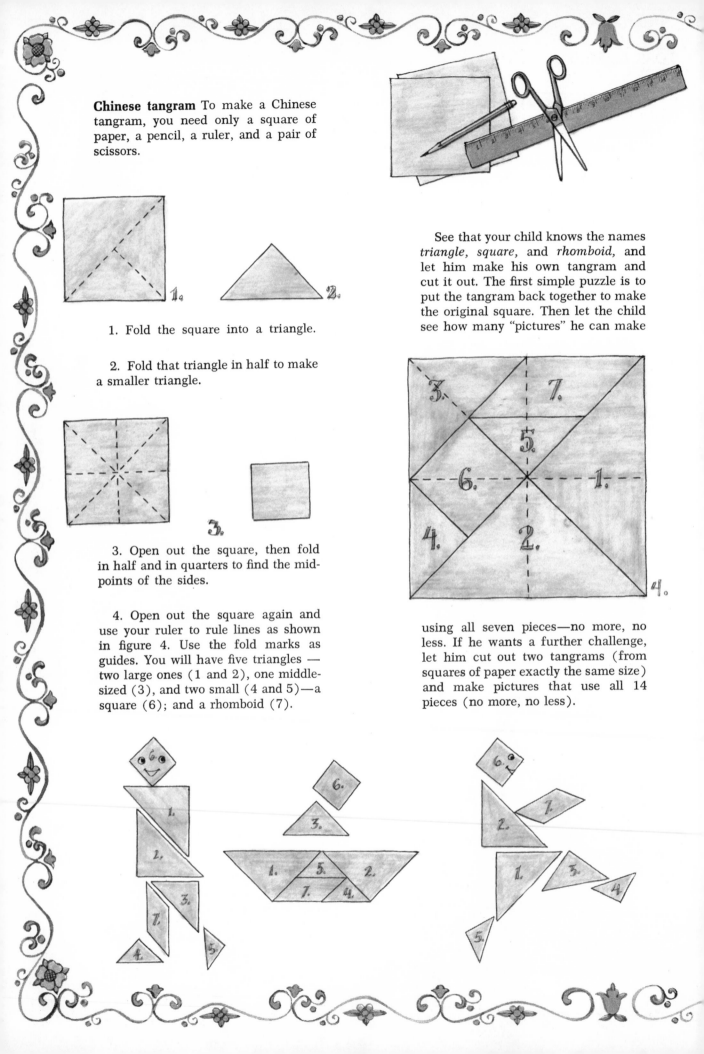

1. Fold the square into a triangle.

2. Fold that triangle in half to make a smaller triangle.

3. Open out the square, then fold in half and in quarters to find the midpoints of the sides.

4. Open out the square again and use your ruler to rule lines as shown in figure 4. Use the fold marks as guides. You will have five triangles — two large ones (1 and 2), one middle-sized (3), and two small (4 and 5)—a square (6); and a rhomboid (7).

See that your child knows the names *triangle, square,* and *rhomboid,* and let him make his own tangram and cut it out. The first simple puzzle is to put the tangram back together to make the original square. Then let the child see how many "pictures" he can make using all seven pieces—no more, no less. If he wants a further challenge, let him cut out two tangrams (from squares of paper exactly the same size) and make pictures that use all 14 pieces (no more, no less).

Stepping through a postcard Ask your patient if he thinks you can step through a postcard. He will be sure you can't. Then show him how to do this trick. Get a used picture post card or government post card. If you have none, get some 5″ x 7″ index cards, and then the child can practice after you've shown him how.

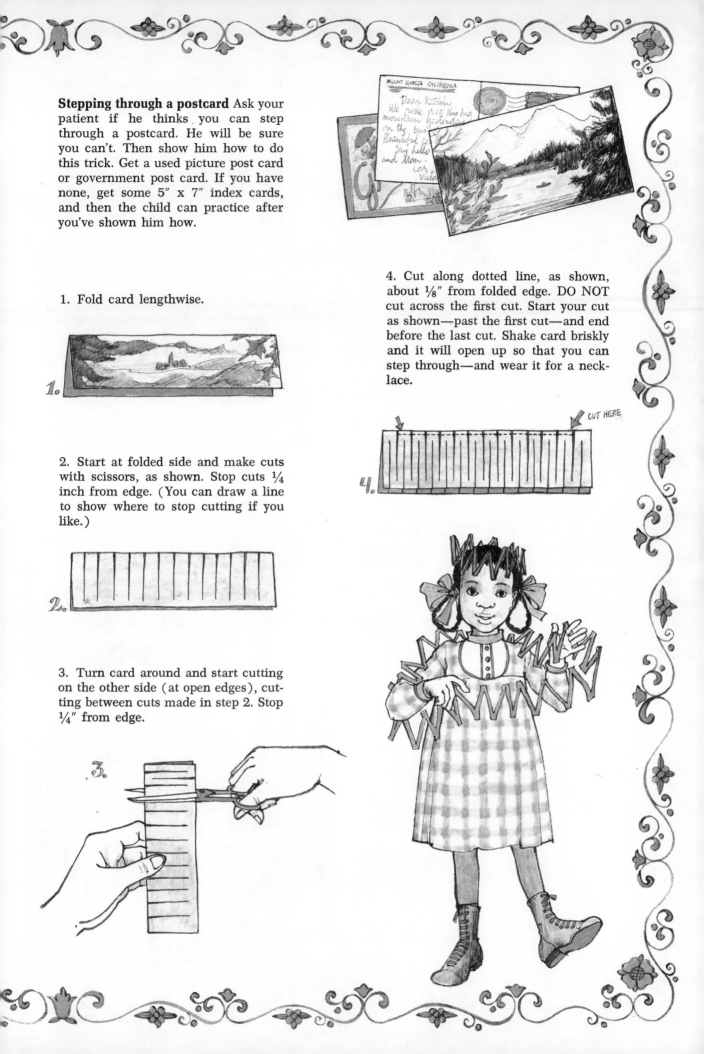

1. Fold card lengthwise.

2. Start at folded side and make cuts with scissors, as shown. Stop cuts ¼ inch from edge. (You can draw a line to show where to stop cutting if you like.)

3. Turn card around and start cutting on the other side (at open edges), cutting between cuts made in step 2. Stop ¼″ from edge.

4. Cut along dotted line, as shown, about ⅛″ from folded edge. DO NOT cut across the first cut. Start your cut as shown—past the first cut—and end before the last cut. Shake card briskly and it will open up so that you can step through—and wear it for a necklace.

CUT HERE

Making a book (See Index.) Make a little book of numbers 1 to 10, with illustrations, for a younger brother or sister. Three sheets of paper folded in half will make 12 pages. Use the front and back for "covers," and you will have 10 pages for the "text." Number the pages. Here are some suggestions for illustrations:

Page 1 — 1 airplane
Page 2 — 2 houses
Page 3 — 3 cars
Page 4 — 4 horses
Page 5 — 5 dogs
Page 6 — 6 cats
Page 7 — 7 flowers
Page 8 — 8 circles (drawn around a penny or button, or freehand)
Page 9 — 9 squares
Page 10 — 10 triangles

Let the child use his imagination, but point out in the beginning that big things must go with low numbers and little things with high numbers, so that there will be room on the pages.

Book Covers These can be used to cover the little books children make, or to cover hardcover books that get lots of use. Use wallpaper sample books if you can get them. Make a pattern out of newspaper, practicing until you get it the way you want it. Then trace the pattern on the wallpaper, and cut it out. Or make the cover out of a brown paper bag, and decorate it with adhesive-backed plastic.

Snowflakes Draw a circle on plain white paper (with a compass or by drawing around a plate). Cut it out. Fold it in half, and then in thirds (because snowflakes have six sides). Cut the top off straight (or leave some rounded). Cut notches of different shapes out of the folded sides and top. Snowflakes can be used as doilies on a tray or pinned to a curtain for decoration.

Clock-watching Give your temporary invalid a clock that doesn't go or isn't wound, and let him set the hands to show the next time he must take his medicine. Then he can tell you when the non-running clock corresponds to the running clock. Or set a timer to make sure. If medicine time is more than an hour, the timer can be reset.

Or let the patient make a play clock with a circle of cardboard or a paper plate. Help him get the numbers in the right places by putting in the 12, 3, 6, and 9 first. Make hands of light cardboard and fasten them on with a paper clasp.

Sign language Give your convalescent a book on sign language — either Indian sign language (page 96) or the language of the deaf. He may want to make up his own sign language. Let him teach you certain signs, and you can take a few minutes now and then to "converse" with him in silent language.

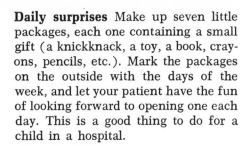

Daily surprises Make up seven little packages, each one containing a small gift (a knickknack, a toy, a book, crayons, pencils, etc.). Mark the packages on the outside with the days of the week, and let your patient have the fun of looking forward to opening one each day. This is a good thing to do for a child in a hospital.

Food surprises When your convalescent is recovering, if there aren't any "no-no's" on his diet, tempt his appetite by having him make a list of his favorite foods. Then surprise him with one at each meal (or one each day if you can't manage one at each meal).

Make a face on a scoop of ice cream, or on a peach or pear half. Use chocolate chips, raisins, or cloves for features.

Occasionally, pack his lunch in a basket or a lunchbox, and call it a picnic.

Work surprises Think up small jobs that the child can do in bed to help you. Show your appreciation when he does. Some of the more interesting jobs could be:

snapping beans for you to cook for dinner,
cleaning out your sewing basket,
making out your grocery list in consultation with you,
straightening up the contents of a desk drawer. (Bring the drawer to him, and give him an empty box for discarding anything he thinks doesn't belong. You can look through the box quickly when the job is done—to check that nothing important has inadvertently been thrown away.)

Surprise visits When the doctor says the child is well enough, surprise him with a visit from a friend.

Covering boxes Covering a small box with decorated adhesive-backed plastic is a good project for a convalescent, for it requires no sticky paste or glue. Make a paper pattern by laying a box on paper and carefully turning it until you have drawn the outlines of all sides. If you want smooth edges, allow for a little "turn-down" on the edges. If the pattern is for a box with a hinged lid, it will look something like this.

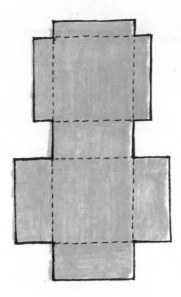

QUICK TRICKS

Bracelets and bubbles String cut-up drinking straws to make a necklace or a bracelet.

Blow soap bubbles (colored with food color).

A box with a separate lid is simpler. Practice with paper until you have what you want. Then trace the pattern on the back of a piece of adhesive-backed plastic, and cut it out. Apply covering slowly and carefully to keep the box smooth and to avoid wrinkles.

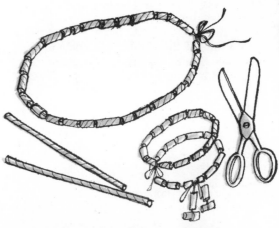

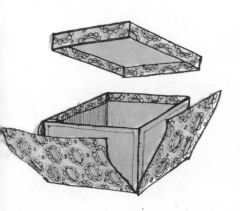

Measuring Give the child a tape measure and a yardstick or a 6-foot rule, and let him take his own measurements—his height, waist, chest, wrists, ankles, etc. He may want to record these important measurements in a notebook, with the date. He may also want to measure his bed, his books, and anything else in sight.

Pictures Make "instant pictures" on the bedspread (or on a tray) with pieces of string or yarn, or buttons.

Remembering Remember a rhyme, a song, a proverb, a quotation, a story. Act one out as far as activity is permitted. (Dolls or toy animals may be substituted for live actors.)

Quotations If the child is old enough, introduce him to a good book of quotations and let him browse.

See:
FAMILIAR QUOTATIONS.
edited by John Bartlett. Little, Brown. 1968.
GOLDEN BOOK OF QUOTATIONS.
Golden, 1970.
THE NEW GOLDEN DICTIONARY.
Golden, 1972.

116

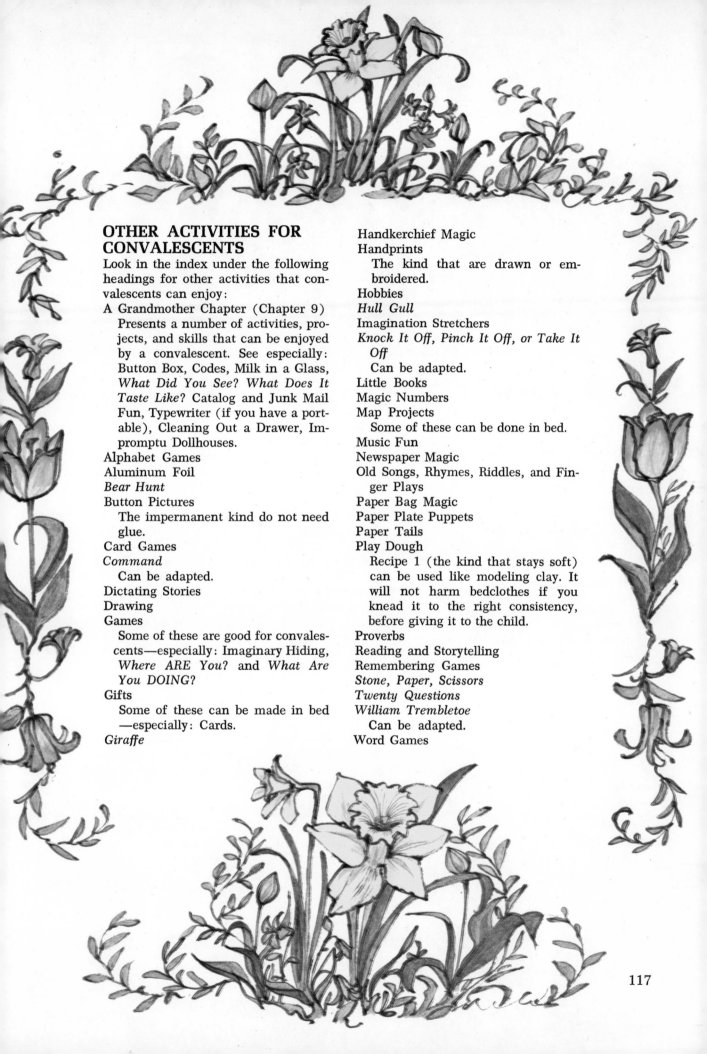

OTHER ACTIVITIES FOR CONVALESCENTS

Look in the index under the following headings for other activities that convalescents can enjoy:

A Grandmother Chapter (Chapter 9)
Presents a number of activities, projects, and skills that can be enjoyed by a convalescent. See especially: Button Box, Codes, Milk in a Glass, *What Did You See? What Does It Taste Like?* Catalog and Junk Mail Fun, Typewriter (if you have a portable), Cleaning Out a Drawer, Impromptu Dollhouses.

Alphabet Games

Aluminum Foil

Bear Hunt

Button Pictures
The impermanent kind do not need glue.

Card Games

Command
Can be adapted.

Dictating Stories

Drawing

Games
Some of these are good for convalescents—especially: Imaginary Hiding, *Where ARE You?* and *What Are You DOING?*

Gifts
Some of these can be made in bed —especially: Cards.

Giraffe

Handkerchief Magic

Handprints
The kind that are drawn or embroidered.

Hobbies

Hull Gull

Imagination Stretchers

Knock It Off, Pinch It Off, or Take It Off
Can be adapted.

Little Books

Magic Numbers

Map Projects
Some of these can be done in bed.

Music Fun

Newspaper Magic

Old Songs, Rhymes, Riddles, and Finger Plays

Paper Bag Magic

Paper Plate Puppets

Paper Tails

Play Dough
Recipe 1 (the kind that stays soft) can be used like modeling clay. It will not harm bedclothes if you knead it to the right consistency, before giving it to the child.

Proverbs

Reading and Storytelling

Remembering Games

Stone, Paper, Scissors

Twenty Questions

William Trembletoe
Can be adapted.

Word Games

Grandmother Chapter

I find myself unable to end this book without including a special chapter for grandmothers. After all, they are the ones who are most likely to have the time and the inclination (and it's important to have both of these at once) to entertain children. They are especially equipped to *enjoy* children — usually, but not always — *grand*children. There are quite a few of what I call proxy grandparents — aunts or uncles, teachers, or other nice people who like children enough to find extra time to explore with them, even when they are not "their own."

"The important thing is to expose children to a multiplicity of activities and interests," says Hughes Mearns in *Creative Power*.* Any adult can add to that "multiplicity" simply by sharing his own enthusiasms; and many go farther, by entering into the spirit of childhood and sharing the enthusiasms of children.

All of my grandmother friends have been exceedingly helpful and enthusiastic about telling me ways in which they enjoy their grandchildren. Louise Thorne, whom I met about the time she retired from teaching, at that time had her full quota of thirteen grandchildren. (That means the number has stayed the same.) My name for her was "The Professional Grandmother," and I consulted her many times. With her snowy hair, pink cheeks, twinkling gray-green eyes, and warm smile, she was the kind of person who would quickly make friends on a train with a young mother traveling with small children. Within an hour, Louise would be sending the mother off to the diner

* *Dover, 1958.*

for a quiet meal, while she entertained the little ones, getting their attention with some toy she just happened to have in her purse.

When I wrote to ask her about activities she enjoyed with her grandchildren, she asked. "Do you mean like taking three of my four families to Williamsburg one year between Christmas and New Year's?" (California was too far for the fourth family to come from.)

I knew about all those grandchildren and their mothers and fathers (Louise has three daughters and a son). Even if one family couldn't come, it made a lot of people! So I answered, "No, indeed! I mean things *any* grandmother could do."

Louise wrote again, "If I could take my children to Williamsburg, anyone can! I took them on money I found I had at the Pittsburgh Teachers' Credit Union, and it was getting only four and a half per cent interest. By spending it in Williamsburg, it created lots more interest.

"The three families drove themselves there, and we had four motel units. I thought each family would have its own quarters, and the few extra children would come in with me; but all the boys wanted to be together, and all the girls with me, and the little ones (three- and four-year-olds) stayed with their parents.

"The girls talked and giggled until all hours, and finally I did mention *cost* — the only time! I said, 'Gramzie is paying over $100 for you to sleep. Now *sleep* — and get our money's worth! Tomorrow we go to James-

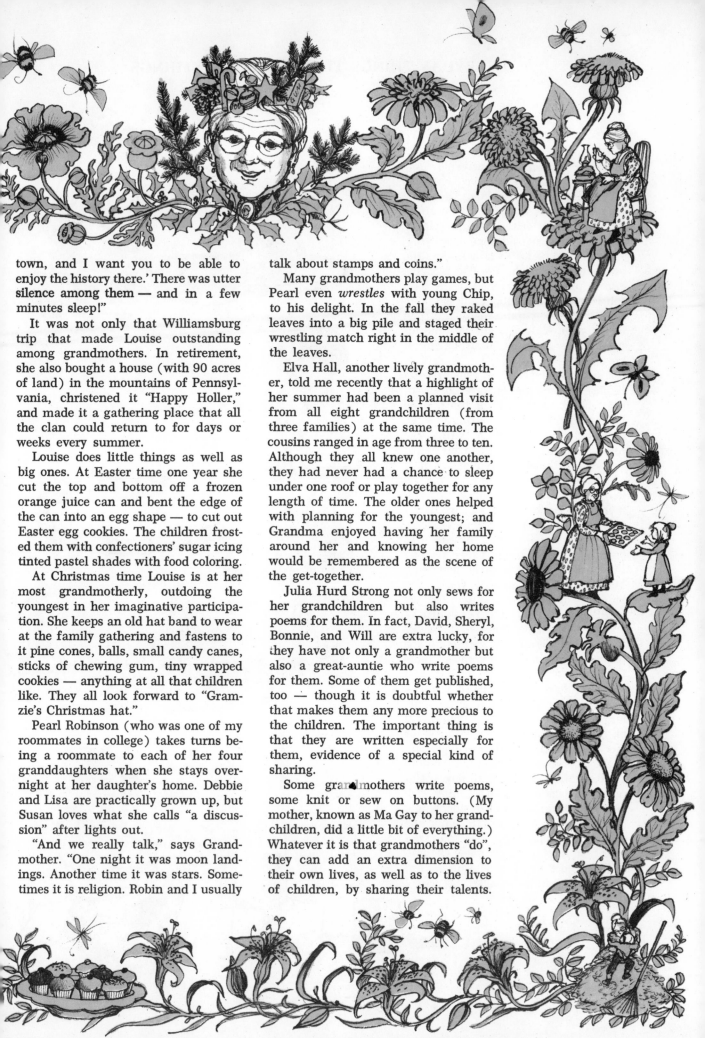

town, and I want you to be able to enjoy the history there.' There was utter silence among them — and in a few minutes sleep!"

It was not only that Williamsburg trip that made Louise outstanding among grandmothers. In retirement, she also bought a house (with 90 acres of land) in the mountains of Pennsylvania, christened it "Happy Holler," and made it a gathering place that all the clan could return to for days or weeks every summer.

Louise does little things as well as big ones. At Easter time one year she cut the top and bottom off a frozen orange juice can and bent the edge of the can into an egg shape — to cut out Easter egg cookies. The children frosted them with confectioners' sugar icing tinted pastel shades with food coloring.

At Christmas time Louise is at her most grandmotherly, outdoing the youngest in her imaginative participation. She keeps an old hat band to wear at the family gathering and fastens to it pine cones, balls, small candy canes, sticks of chewing gum, tiny wrapped cookies — anything at all that children like. They all look forward to "Gramzie's Christmas hat."

Pearl Robinson (who was one of my roommates in college) takes turns being a roommate to each of her four granddaughters when she stays overnight at her daughter's home. Debbie and Lisa are practically grown up, but Susan loves what she calls "a discussion" after lights out.

"And we really talk," says Grandmother. "One night it was moon landings. Another time it was stars. Sometimes it is religion. Robin and I usually talk about stamps and coins."

Many grandmothers play games, but Pearl even *wrestles* with young Chip, to his delight. In the fall they raked leaves into a big pile and staged their wrestling match right in the middle of the leaves.

Elva Hall, another lively grandmother, told me recently that a highlight of her summer had been a planned visit from all eight grandchildren (from three families) at the same time. The cousins ranged in age from three to ten. Although they all knew one another, they had never had a chance to sleep under one roof or play together for any length of time. The older ones helped with planning for the youngest; and Grandma enjoyed having her family around her and knowing her home would be remembered as the scene of the get-together.

Julia Hurd Strong not only sews for her grandchildren but also writes poems for them. In fact, David, Sheryl, Bonnie, and Will are extra lucky, for they have not only a grandmother but also a great-auntie who write poems for them. Some of them get published, too — though it is doubtful whether that makes them any more precious to the children. The important thing is that they are written especially for them, evidence of a special kind of sharing.

Some grandmothers write poems, some knit or sew on buttons. (My mother, known as Ma Gay to her grandchildren, did a little bit of everything.) Whatever it is that grandmothers "do", they can add an extra dimension to their own lives, as well as to the lives of children, by sharing their talents.

Most grandmothers discovered long ago that a baby loves to have a couple of cooking pans with lids. The noise may be too much after a few minutes, and then you can substitute plastic cups that stack inside one another.

Playing with water is a fascinating occupation. Jerry used to like a plastic cup or pitcher and funnel in the bath tub, and he would play endlessly with the garden hose and a dishpan or pail in the yard. Making a special time for water play is better than having it occur by accident.

Cardboard tubes from rolls of toilet tissue or paper towels have dozens of uses. Mike, at the age of three, liked to have them tied on a string (tie the first one, and then simply "string" the rest) to make a "snake" to be pulled around the house as happily as if it were a "store-bought" pull-toy. Stephanie, at five, liked to help make little animal candy baskets out of them. Here's how: Cut the tube into 2-inch sections. Use each section for a basket. Use crepe paper or ordinary paper to cover the cardboard and to make a bottom. Make faces to paste on the front (rabbit for Easter, Santa for Christmas, boy or girl for a birthday, etc. For Fourth of July use a whole toilet tissue tube. Paint it red (or cover it with red crepe paper) to make giant firecracker table favors.

Cereal boxes (Julia Hurd reminds me of the small, one-serving size), detergent boxes, any kind of boxes, big or little, are excellent substitutes for blocks. Stuff crumpled newspapers into the boxes to make them a little more durable. Make a town with boxes. Cut up paper bags for the street. Line various-sized boxes up on each side. Name the buildings—the store, the bank, the school, the church, houses. For the youngest, naming the boxes is enough. A little older child may want to use crayons or paints to make the school *look* like a school, etc.

Button box Because grandmother can give the little one her undivided attention, she may be able to let a baby play with buttons earlier than mother can. Sorting (big and little) stringing, making "streets" on the floor, making buttons "rain"—these are all fun for the very young at different stages of development. You can introduce marbles, tiles, coins, and nails this way if you are prepared to stay on the scene and keep on the alert to see that nothing goes into eyes, ears, nose, or mouth. Talk about what you are doing. Name things. If you can't be on the spot to maintain *constant* supervision, skip anything dangerous (like nails).

Learning how things work Grandfathers are often good at introducing little ones to tools. A young child loves to open and close hinged boxes; put lids on and off shoe boxes; operate a light switch; use a key; ring a doorbell; dial a telephone number; operate snaps, hooks, and catches; set a timer.

Save an old clock for your grandson to take apart. Let him keep the parts in his own special box.

Give a three-year-old your discarded costume jewelry to carry around in a cigar box when she isn't dressing up in it.

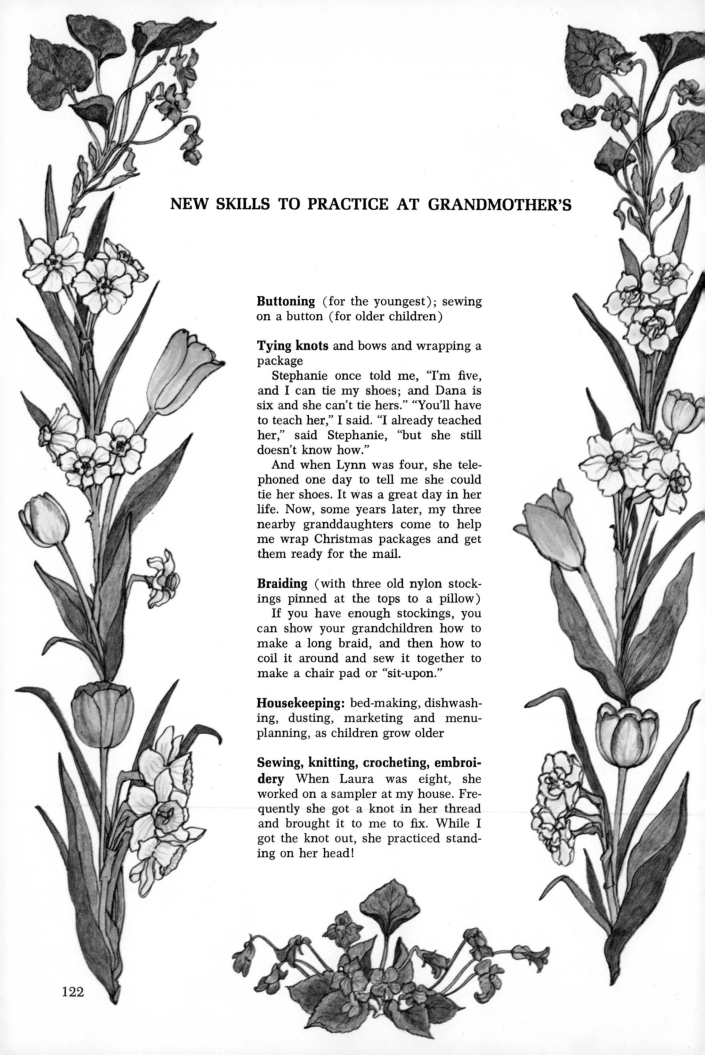

NEW SKILLS TO PRACTICE AT GRANDMOTHER'S

Buttoning (for the youngest); sewing on a button (for older children)

Tying knots and bows and wrapping a package

Stephanie once told me, "I'm five, and I can tie my shoes; and Dana is six and she can't tie hers." "You'll have to teach her," I said. "I already teached her," said Stephanie, "but she still doesn't know how."

And when Lynn was four, she telephoned one day to tell me she could tie her shoes. It was a great day in her life. Now, some years later, my three nearby granddaughters come to help me wrap Christmas packages and get them ready for the mail.

Braiding (with three old nylon stockings pinned at the tops to a pillow)

If you have enough stockings, you can show your grandchildren how to make a long braid, and then how to coil it around and sew it together to make a chair pad or "sit-upon."

Housekeeping: bed-making, dishwashing, dusting, marketing and menu-planning, as children grow older

Sewing, knitting, crocheting, embroidery When Laura was eight, she worked on a sampler at my house. Frequently she got a knot in her thread and brought it to me to fix. While I got the knot out, she practiced standing on her head!

Lighting a match and a candle; laying a fire in the fireplace and lighting it (with supervision, of course).

Fish face Everybody ought to know how to do this, and very young children love to try getting their mouths into this position. Wiggling the lower lip makes a "fish kiss" or "fish talk."

Butterfly kiss Ask a child if she wants a butterfly kiss. If she says yes, bat your eyelashes against her cheek, then against the back of her hand so she can see how you do it.

SPECIAL PROJECTS
FOR GRANDMOTHERS

Calendar towels When you have a new grandchild, get a calendar towel for that year. Embroider on it the new baby's name, and a circle around his birthday. If there is room, add his birth weight. Then put the towel away, and give it to the child when he is old enough to appreciate it (or give it to his mother to keep).

Sugar plum tree A sugar plum tree can be made to serve as a centerpiece for any table on any special occasion. Get the end of a tree branch from your yard. Stick small gum drops on the ends of the twigs, and stand the "tree" in a flower holder or a flower pot.

YOU CAN USE MARSHMALLOWS TOO!

VARIATION Cut squares of tissue paper. Pat a small wad of crumpled paper in the middle of each square. Pull the tissue paper up around the filling, and tie with gaily colored string. Put into ball shapes, and tie on your little tree. (These ornaments can be used on a Christmas tree. Practice with several squares to get the sizes you want.)

File folders Keep a manila envelope or file folder with data about grandchildren—letters or pictures they give you, clippings you want to send them, a list of favorite foods or special interests, etc. If you can remember to do it, record your grandchildren's "bright sayings." These are quickly forgotten, but they love to hear about them a year or two later.

FOR A FARAWAY GRANDMOTHER

Keep records of grandchildren's measurements. Ask your daughter or daughter-in-law to send you updated measurements two or three times a year, so that when you go shopping you won't buy clothes that are too small.

Save letters and pictures children send you. Hazel La Fever saves Christmas cards that show pictures of her friends' families. Five or ten years later, mother and father may have a copy of the card, but their growing-up children have none and are delighted to get the old picture back.

Send a code to your grandchild, and write him a short message in code.

Here is an easy code to remember.

Here is a message in the code — and its translation.

Dear Jud,
You are invited to my house for strawberry shortcake on Tuesday after school. Linda and Nancie are coming too. Love, Grammie

Send little things in letters:
Paper dolls
Paper boats
Gummed stars
Band-Aids
A homemade puzzle made from a bright postcard
A rhyme
Stamps or postcards to start (or add to) a collection
A riddle (with the answer folded up on a separate sheet of paper)
A clipping about his hobby
A Chinese tangram, with directions for making it
Snapshots
Heart baskets made from corners of used envelopes

SPECIAL GRANDMOTHER GAMES

William Trembletoe and *Knock It Off, Pinch It Off, or Take It Off* (see Index) are very ancient games, borrowed from a grandmother's grandmother. Here is another game that bridges the generation gap.

Milk in a Glass Stand behind your grandchild, facing the same direction he faces. Hold up any number of fingers from one to five, and repeat this rhyme,

Milk in a glass, tea in a cup,
How many fingers do I hold up?

If the child guesses the right answer, you say, "Two you said (or three, or whatever), and two there were." Then change places with him, whereupon *he* says the rhyme and holds up fingers, and *you* guess. (If he guessed wrong, you say, "Three you said, and two there were." Quickly repeat the question and go on with the game until he guesses correctly.) If several children are present, grandmother can ask the rhyming question, with the children taking turns in front of her.

SENSORY GAMES

In addition to the sensory games mentioned on page 58, try these:

What Did You See? Put ten or twelve common objects: a button, a toothbrush, a pencil, a leaf, a rock, an apple, an orange, etc., on a tray. Let the child count them and look at them for a minute or two. Then cover the tray with a towel, and ask how many she can remember.

What Does It Taste Like? Introduce children to four basic tastes — sweet, sour, salty, bitter. They may not care to taste "bitter," but if they do, raw cocoa and vanilla are good examples. Children are always amazed at the difference between the taste and the smell of vanilla.

Make up any kind of tasting game you like. One game is to have a child close or cover his eyes; then let him taste what you put to his lips, and name it. Foods used could be a bit of salted cracker, a teaspoonful of orange juice, a drop or two of vinegar or lemon juice, a piece of fudge, a wedge of raw carrot, a bite of hard-boiled egg, a bit of sugar. Show the child all the foods before he closes his eyes.

TREASURE HUNT

For a successful treasure hunt, it usually takes longer to prepare the clues than it does for the children to find them, read them, and make their way to the treasure. For this reason, a wise grandmother will suggest that the children (if they are old enough to write) prepare the clues and hide them in rooms or the yard or wherever she designates. The treasure can be anything from a bag of cookies to a jump rope. Three or four clues are enough.

If only one child is present, he will enjoy having grandmother make the hunt. In this case, the child can think up the treasure, or he can ask grandmother to supply a surprise.

CATALOG AND JUNK MAIL FUN

When John and Kathy and Jimmy and Jean were very young, their Mimi saved her junk mail in a special drawer that they could open when they came to visit. Opening it was part of the fun, and they had their own ways of re-cycling junk. They cut out pictures to put in a scrap book, or to paste on a book cover or box. They also liked to cut paper into small pieces of various shapes and colors to cover cottage cheese cartons, pill boxes, and other containers. Later these were sprayed with clear varnish or spray starch, to give a smooth finish.

A new catalog can be a wish book, and a good game can be played by asking the question, "If you could have only one thing in this whole catalog, what would it be?"

Let your grandchild select a birth-day or Christmas present (within a certain price range) from a catalog. Show him how to make out an order. Seal it, stamp it, and take it to the post office.

When a catalog is out of date, it can be used in the same way as junk mail.

CLEANING OUT A DRAWER

When you let a child help you clean out a drawer, what might be a tiresome chore becomes an adventure. The drawer *gives* all sorts of things that the very young have new eyes for . . . that tiny box you no longer have use for, a discarded piece of jewelry, a little artificial flower, the ruffle you cut off an old dress, a hotel cake of soap in its wrapper. Of course, you can't clean out the same drawer too often; it can't continue to give in the same way — unless it has time to accumulate new treasure. But there are many drawers in a house, and they offer opportunities for useful (from the point of view of your Puritan conscience) activity that can be fun when it is shared.

TYPEWRITER

A typewriter is fascinating to a small child, especially when he is learning the alphabet. Even a three-year-old will enjoy it for a little while, with a minimum of supervision. I have found that my grandchildren do no harm to the typewriter, but I insist that they take turns solo. There is no satisfactory way to play a duet on a typewriter.

IMPROMPTU DOLLHOUSES

A visiting granddaughter may have a real dollhouse at home, but a dollhouse improvised on the spur of the moment can be more fun than any other kind. Provide a box (turned on one side, so that it is open in front and closed on all other sides), or just use a book shelf.

Make furniture out of objects found around the house, such as:

a round table from a circle of cardboard pasted on a large spool

stools for the table from smaller spools

a bed from a small box

sheets from handkerchiefs or small scraps of cloth

lamp shades, flower pots, etc., from different-sized toothpaste caps and other kinds of tops

pictures from magazines to hang on the walls

Lynn, Laura, and Stephanie have book-shelf dollhouses that they have enjoyed for years. In them they have a mixture of furnishings made by themselves, made by their mother, bought at stores, and given to them as gifts. I think perhaps they have enjoyed the things made by themselves the most. (Maybe Alice creates her own Wonderland.)

I still remember the pleasure Helen Sheriff, my only lifelong friend, and I had with our box dollhouses. The boxes were made of wood, and it seems they lasted for years as our interest in them came and went. We even piled them on a wagon one day and took them to the park to give them new surroundings. I don't recall that we had anything "boughten" in our dollhouses; I suppose our homemade furnishings were crude, but to us they were fascinating.

QUICK TRICKS FOR GRANDMOTHER TO SUGGEST

Play *Tiddlywinks* with buttons.

Make pictures on the floor with string or yarn.

Draw or paint a picture.

Make a mural on the refrigerator with homemade finger paint. (See Index.)

Dictate a story for grandmother to keep. (See Index.)

Act out a rhyme, proverb, or story.

Sing a song.

Make quick cookies.

Dress up in grandmother's clothes.

Make a train (a pull-toy) by fastening milk cartons together with string.

Make a train (child-size) by lining up chairs.

Take a picture.

Make a gift for somebody.

Make a Chinese tangram. (See Index.)

Play a card game.

Make holiday decorations.

Make paper dolls and stuff them. Make clothes for them. Name them. (See Index.)

Make a sailboat out of a cork, a straight pin, and a paper sail.

Drape a sheet over a table to make a house.

Make a snake (a pull-toy) by stringing cardboard tubes from toilet tissue.

Make a village with different-sized boxes for the buildings. (See Index.)

Mix a little egg yolk with a little dry detergent and food color to make the color stick to shiny surfaces like egg cartons, foil, glass, or refrigerators.

Play *Tenpins* with plastic bottles.

Step through a postcard. (See Index.)

Play store.

Play school.

Clean out a drawer.

Make impromptu dollhouses.

Take a walk.

GRANDMOTHER'S TREASURE CHEST

If you enjoy children, it is easy to build up a treasure chest of raw materials for them to make things with. The treasure chest can be anything from a big box to an extra closet. If you purchase items, try to buy things that help children create.

Some things worth saving

egg cartons
plastic bottles
pill bottles
inner tubes
cardboard tubes from toilet tissue and
    paper towels
remnants of cloth, lace, braid, etc.
rags
old nylon stockings
cotton
scraps of wood, linoleum, tile, carpet,
    etc.
corks
tin cans
pieces of candles
boxes of all kinds
corrugated paper
tissue paper and cleansing tissues
spools
buttons
sandpaper
nut shells
paper clips
old crayons
paper bags
newspapers and magazines
old toothbrushes (for spatter painting
    and for scrubbing)

Some things worth buying

paints
crayons
chalk
art materials
felt
glue
hobby materials
nylon net
plaster of Paris
clay
wire
wood
felt markers
adhesive-backed plastic

A LAST WORD

There are no cross references for this Grandmother Chapter, because I hope grandparents will want to explore *all* of this book's chapters when they have opportunities to enjoy children. More than that, I hope they will think of activities that I have omitted: a special family tradition or custom, a childhood song or story or game, a specialized skill or interest or hobby that they want to make a part of their grandchildren's heritage. The future grows out of the past, and grandparents are in a good position to pass on the best of what they remember to the third generation.

On the next page you can begin to jot down notes for your own book, and in the meantime enjoy this one!

NOTES

NOTES

INDEX

ABCDEFGHIJ